ADOLESCENCE
AND STRESS

Dr Faith Spicer MB, BS

FORBES PUBLICATIONS

© Forbes Publications Limited
All rights reserved
First published 1977 ISBN 0 901762 27 X

Forbes Publications Limited
Hartree House, Queensway, London W2 4SH
*Printed in Great Britain by
Chapel River Press, Andover, Hants.*

Contents

Introduction

This book is not a 'teach yourself counselling' manual. It is designed to offer more a philosophy than a creed. It does not pretend either to be based upon rigid scientific criteria nor upon absolute knowledge. I have, over the years, been well aware that the word 'counselling' has become very imprecise and that a mystique has arisen around it that may be more obscurantist than useful to put it mildly. The time has almost certainly come when a word, be it counselling or something else, should be used to define a very real technique which is neither 'good advice' nor psychotherapy.

Throughout the country there are a number of courses which teach the skills of counselling to members of many disciplines: some of the students are teachers, some are social workers, doctors, future marriage guidance counsellors. Each student will use a common skill in different environments. There are now very many 'Counselling Centres' both for adolescents and for adults. Some of them are excellent, some less so. Some are staffed mostly by volunteers, both trained and untrained, some by salaried individuals. There is a growing literature concerning this skill. Soon it may be possible to be far more precise as to the value of different techniques and different training courses.

I have written this book for another group of professionals, professionals whose unique and extensive contact with children gives them skills of a very special high order. Apart from parents there are very few people who have such long-continued experience of growing children as teachers, so that it would be an impertinence on my part to pretend that I know children better.

But because we now recognize that teaching involves some recognition of differences in pupils and that the mood of the pupil can be as important as his intelligence in his ability to gain from teaching; because in a shifting and rapidly changing society we have to help young people to be more, rather than less, self-reliant, more able to choose and to decide, more able to argue and to think, more able to be democratic, then the teacher must need to understand, if possible, the distressing, often infuriating, behaviour of her pupils.

I am quite certain that if teachers involve themselves more in the understanding of children, then life becomes harder for them but it also becomes more fun, more invigorating and more worthwhile.

If a class is not intimidated into silence then it won't always be quiet, the borderline between control and chaos will be more difficult to establish. If a teacher attempts to reach a little nearer to her pupils' personalities, she will receive more rebuffs as well as more satisfying work. She will need a greater understanding of adolescence, a greater acceptance of her own sense of failure, a greater ability to recognize that she doesn't know all the answers. She will also need to preserve confidentiality and come up against more conflicting loyalties. What she won't need to be is a counsellor.

I think it would do no service whatsoever to school-children if all staff saw themselves as counsellors. For one thing it would, quite likely, be seen by the pupils as a gross invasion of privacy. For another, the teacher would lose her main and uniquely important function – that of teaching, and the encouragement of her pupils' development. This book is, primarily, written perhaps to shed a very faint light upon the more puzzling young person, the pupil who is a surprise or an anxiety, who doesn't behave as expected.

I don't think teachers always feel very secure about their capabilities. My own very strong view is that it's time everyone stopped colluding in scape-goating them for all the problems of adolescents. Adolescents are always going to be pretty frightful, certainly the condition of adolescence is not a disease and certainly only a very few of them need either counselling or psychotherapy. Not only that, but they don't need to be, never can be, nor even want to be, understood. If teachers feel more confident about their own skills I reckon the children in their care will be happier and easier. This book is written as a tribute to the many teachers who spend their lives assisting in the maturation process of our awkward young.

CHAPTER 1

Early childhood and the family

This book will be concentrating upon the counselling needs of adolescents, but before this area of the child's life is explored it might be sensible to look in two ways at children's development and problems before that time.

It is becoming more and more apparent that the early life of the child will determine to a great extent how he responds to adolescence and, perhaps more cogently, teachers, police, social workers and parents themselves; that is, all those in direct and intimate contact with children are now confronted with very clear signs that behaviour problems are occurring at a younger age. One measure of this is seen in the fact that truanting is now becoming a moderately common phenomenon in the Infant School, another lies in the delinquency figures and a third in the child guidance findings and complaints of teachers and parents.

I intend later on to deal briefly with some areas of child development, but at present would like to have a look at a few pointers which might lead one to be able to agree that plenty is known and recorded about the effects of differing levels of mothering and fathering upon the child.

There is a good deal of literature concerning this and the Newsome's study[1] and that of the Birmingham Project for Under-Fives[2] are two examples, but I would like to describe some experiences of my own to illustrate my point.

I am sitting at a desk in an Infant Welfare Clinic. A mother comes in with a baby and starts to talk to me. The mother, as she talks fondles the baby's head, occasionally changes its position, often smiles at the baby while talking to me, even interrupts her own flow of conversation to croon a little to him and then to talk to me. Another mother comes in. This time she is perhaps rather fidgety and strained, she has the baby in her arms and rocks it to and fro putting it up to her chest then putting it down, looking at me, then at the baby, and gradually making *me* feel fidgety and ill at ease. The baby is restless and cries and we all feel fretful. A third mother comes in with her baby who is in a carrycot and just stays in the cot while we talk, to be brought out

1

for me to examine. When the baby is to be dressed she asks me if she can use the table to lie it on so that she can organize the nappy properly.

Already we have three sorts of mothering. If I see these three mothers on and off for a year or so, I will see three differing progressions. I will suppose for the moment, which is absurd, that all the babies were born the same.

The first mother will come in with her child, perhaps walking by now. As she comes in she may remark to her child something about me and the room and show some of my toys to the baby. The baby herself will also look round and move toward the toys in an enquiring manner. Perhaps the child will initially show some anxiety about me, but the mother, sensing this, will be soothing and encouraging and will co-operate with me in helping the child to feel at home in the room. The child will then explore the toys and perhaps be able to make friends with me and we shall all three become friends together.

The second child may come in very fretful and a bit frightened. The mother will apologize and tell the child not to be silly. Toys will be brought out, the child continues to cry, promises be given, apologies made, and the child, rather thin and pale, will take some time to claim down.

The third child may come in and sit very quietly, but seeing the toys, may move toward them, the mother in the middle of talking to me will almost automatically say, 'Don't touch, it's not yours' and go on speaking to me. The child will give up and continue to sit quietly.

It does not take three descriptions for it to be established that the effect of mothering upon the child is crucial in determining not only the development of self-esteem and behaviour, but also of the vital areas of enquiry, trust and learning, because without enquiry and trust, learning cannot take place. Would it be possible to predict the future of these children? And would it be profitable? Yes, of course, on both counts. It has been established over and over again that by one year of age children brought up in a home where enquiry is encouraged are intellectually both manually and verbally ahead of those not given this sort of environment. More crucial even than this are the studies that have been done to show the differing effects of anxious (or neurotic), cold, and loving mothering. If one could predict varying effects of different levels of mothering what would one find? The major types of problem that beset the child and adult might be categorized in various ways. One would be to define behaviour in terms of normality, neurosis or delinquency. Or one could measure the verbal ability, manual dexterity, sensory perception and so on. Many studies of children have reinforced our own experience and perception of this.

In a study in America of deprived children[3] at the pre-school level, it was seen that the children were behind in verbal skills (though at first, paradoxically, they might seem to *talk* much more freely it could be observed that the conversations were strangely sterile and unrelated to the situation). They were physically much more clumsy, both in fine movements of the figures and hands and in balancing and dancing. Their ability to hold an interest in a task was much curtailed, and indeed their performance level was lower. Another factor which would be of immense importance for their future would be their very labile emotional levels. The children would get angry and impatient quicker, change mood rapidly, contain their frustration less ably, and, although sometimes apparently caring for their friends would only do so at an oddly inconsequential level (rather as though acting the part of an adult). Their ability to play was also very superficial. They could not use fantasy in play and 'pretend' to be mother and father, or nurses or policemen, but could really only dart to and fro shouting or sit in a corner doing very little. Relationships with adults were different also. They would rapidly approach, apparently being very friendly and confiding, but rush away again – so that they seemed unable to see adults as real and could not make relationships in depth. Comparable studies have shown similar results. All teachers are familiar with this situation and one of the first tasks of schooling in these cases would be to build up relationships and develop ability to play and use fantasy.

It is this group of children who we see again in adolescence with multiple behaviour problems, traunting, violence, non-performing, sexually promiscuous perhaps, delinquent and hostile, whose ability to hold frustration is minimal, whose need for instant gratification is overpowering, whose ability to see other people's needs as of any value is minimal, who cannot hold down a job, because it is boring, or because of bad time-keeping, bad behaviour, bad language, who if they marry may beat their wives, neglect or batter their children. It all sounds very gloomy.

3

Some years ago, when still working in Maternity and Child Welfare Clinics, I and a colleague tried hard to establish some kind of 'at risk' register for children. We hoped that if we could defined certain family situations as being potentially damaging to children and enable Health Visitors, doctors and other people in contact with them to be alert to their vulnerability it might be possible to avert some of the damage or, if not, at least to recognize the beginning of a problem as early as possible. For one reason or another at that time the project did not get any further, but a year or so later, when working in a boys' school in another project seeking to identify the needs and problems of school-leavers, I used the register we had devised retrospectively to look at the records of all the boys leaving in a particular year. Briefly we had listed factors of the following kind:

Absence by death or desertion of father or mother

Absence for long periods through work or illness of either parent

Severe and prolonged illness or neurosis in either partner

Severe or prolonged illness in a sibling

Long-term hospitalization in client.

In looking at the records of the boys we decided to count as positive signs of distress that a Care Committee Worker in the school had made regular visits to the home. She would have attended if the child were to be assessed for free dinners, for appointments at hospitals, for truanting at school, or if the parents or teachers were troubled in some way. We also looked at those children who had attended juvenile court.

We found that over 80 per cent of the children with positive 'at risk' factors had in fact been known to the Care Committee Worker, and only 20 per cent of those with no 'at risk' factor were known; we also noticed (and this has also been documented elsewhere) that the difficulties had in most cases shown up in the Infant School as well.

Various studies of delinquency patterns of children[4] have high-lighted the fact that family size (over four children) is very highly correlated with delinquency.

Therefore, if we could, by making use of knowledge already present, modify our systems of care for these highly vulnerable children *from the moment of birth*, then a number of late-school problems might be avoided. It might also be that teaching could be made a more pleasurable task. Deprived children are empty, angry, superficial, non-caring and uninterested. They have not had the primary good experience with the parents, as I have suggested, either to build enquiry or trust. Not only that, but they have not incorporated, through identification *with* parents, a good image of either adults or themselves. I shall come back to this later, but want to examine this situation in this chapter as well, as I think it has relevance. If the child has not been talked *to*, listened *to*, cared *for*, has never been really wanted or loved; if his enquiring fingers have been slapped and if his emotions have never been accepted, then of *course* learning of all sort is boring, people untrustworthy, words useless, of *course* violence is the only way to free himself of frustration and anguish, pain and fury. No child can be expected to *enjoy* the discipline of learning and sharing and the curbing of frustration if he has never experienced the normal pattern of childhood and the development of personal self-esteem. The boys I worked with, all aged 15, were loud-mouthed, angry, delinquent, almost illiterate, promiscuous and selfish, but they also were frightened of their feeling of inadequacy, their sense of being 'put down', unwanted, thrown on the heap. However good the teaching, these boys would find it almost impossible to break the barrier of their mistrust of themselves as well as of 'them', to move into a useful learning situation.

Girls in a comparable situation are almost more of a puzzle. They seem totally uninterested in anything. In Youth Clubs they sit about saying nothing, turn aside when approached, appear unaware of the friendly advances of youth leaders or the boys. They are sullen, restless, bored. I've no doubt in school they sit at the back, make up, giggle, fidget and seem totally uncaring. Both groups see school as useless, home as useless, and society as useless. But if you *do* find a way to talk to them, and *do* take them seriously and listen, they will in fact, as trust gradually emerges, voice their opinions, show their anxieties, find interest in discussion. Their expectations are low. I asked a group of 15-year-olds what they wanted to do when they left school. None had any aspirations at all – 'work in a shop', 'work in an office', 'my Auntie will get me a place in her factory'. None thought it worthwhile to continue to study for a higher goal, though a few admitted typing would be good. Their attitude to life was that you worked for a bit, saved a bit, and got married. They had no ambition to marry an educated man, or a man 'going places', they said the one would scare them and the other make them feel they couldn't keep up. They didn't want a good looking man as they expected him not to be trustworthy. Their greatest aim was to find a man who was a good worker and brought his wages home regularly. Interestingly enough the boys thought the same. They didn't want a good-looker, they thought she would be a roamer and hard to keep. They also thought she'd be a bad housewife and mother.

Both groups, for all their hostility and bragging, were feeling pretty inadequate. We took them to a theatre and the journey across London made them most uneasy, a few pretended they knew the way. They didn't like the theatre, it meant looking ahead, demanded manners they didn't feel they had, and an acceptance of the format of the staging which seemed to them nonsensical. One boy had never crossed the main road half a mile from his school so that attendance at a Child Guidance Clinic was impossible. He got so lost he landed at the local police station which upset him and his family no end. Another had not seen the river, though he lived within two miles of it. Some of the group had, in fact, found a fishing spot in the country by a canal. An old gent up there had helped them with a hut, and they used to go regularly to fish – 'it's peaceful up there', they said 'nice and quiet and away from everyone'. Another had been to Cheddar Gorge once and described the eeriness of the place as it got dark – 'and the fog, like, it came up the sides of the place and it was really weird – you felt miles from anywhere – quite weird it was, I was quite scared, and so quiet, but nice really. I'll never forget it'. They loved their own area 'Well, it's friendly I mean you know everyone – you know, nice and noisy and plenty going on'.

Some of their friends had moved to a new town and although they acknowledged that it was clean and at least everyone had enough room, yet they thought it was awful. 'Well, there's nothing to do for a start – the road's empty at night – the place is dead – there's no faces, no night life and even in the day, well it's dead. I couldn't live there even if it did give us more room'. These boys had two absolute dislikes and very many prejudices. Nothing could shake their dislike of the police. 'They get to know you, and you can't step outside your door, but they're after you; every time you ride your bike they stop you and say it's not yours, every time you walk down the market – "Ere, what are you after then?" – once you've been to court they never leave you alone – and the courts, you never get your rights there, they tell such lies'. If asked 'Why not plead Not Guilty and get a fair hearing?' they jeered 'Who's going to listen to one of us, then, when he's up there telling lies all the time and your mum and dad's moaning at the waste of time sitting there, or mum's crying 'er eyes out, thinking you'll go away, you'll get guilty in the end any road, so you might as well save time and say it to start with – nobody will listen'.

Their second hate is weak 'useless' teachers. 'If he's got something to teach us, why doesn't he get on with it then?' 'Why does he go on and on talking a load of rubbish, all right so we've got to be at school, why can't he teach us something, 'stead of trying to make friends or something all the time and then losing 'is temper?' They wanted a man who was fair, strict and made them feel contained – 'silly b...., he just makes us laugh, then we fool around, then there's hell to pay – it's all his fault for being so wet'.

Their housing is often awful – David lived in one room with his mother and a series of 'Uncles'. His main hatred was of homosexuals. He was, himself, a good looking lad, had no father, and was clearly suffering quite considerably from his own unacknowledged fears.

Jack lived with his mother and father, one brother and three sisters in a three roomed flat. The father had built partitions so that the boys and girls were separate. Jack said that you had to stand on the bed to dress and that the boarding was so thin you could hear everything – 'well' he said, 'I mean, it's not very nice with your sister within touching, I mean, you get thoughts don't you – it's not right, really – and then one day' he said 'I was walking through the kitchen, right? and my mum she was at the sink, having a wash – well, there she was, stripped to the waist, her great tits swinging to and fro and me watching – well, it was awful, I can't forget that – I mean you shouldn't have to watch a thing like that'. Jack was perhaps one of the most difficult boys in the school, he threw whatever came to hand from top-floor windows at masters down below (but, fortunately, never hit one), was constantly in trouble, was a coward when caned by the Head, was disruptive and thoroughly disliked. His sexual fantasies worried him deeply, he described a number of them to us – all putting women in humbling and hurtful situations – but perhaps his ability to talk helped him. His behaviour certainly improved and when he left school he very much enjoyed his job as a butcher's boy.

They all condemned homosexuality, partly, because many of them had been involved in episodes round the area; men would offer them money to come with them, and it frightened them very much, particularly as eventually one man committed suicide.

They were extremely prejudiced about the blacks, who were allegedly responsible for the housing shortage, and took all the best jobs and girls and ran all the brothels and owned the biggest cars. But among them were several coloured boys whom they liked and were totally friendly with, and they had a great admiration for several well-known coloured athletes, dentists and youth leaders.

I think one must be careful in recording the aspirations and attitudes of these boys not to confuse those that stemmed from a perfectly ordinary and quite rich working class culture, a culture different from mine, but none the less warm, supportive and friendly, though perhaps constricting and not highly verbal and intellectual or aspiring, and those that were as a result of parti-cular circumstances in some of them. It would be monstrous and patently absurd to define as deprived, hostile, maladjusted, boys who simply didn't talk, behave or want the same as myself or a teacher. It would also be absurd not to recognize that upon these children there are influences that are in fact stultifying and damaging.

Overcrowding does not only happen because you are inade-quate, though a number of inadequate people are living in overcrowded conditions, but overcrowding does set its own patterns. The overcrowded family cannot afford *not* to have stronger sexual taboos, *has* to develop ways of not communicating, of showing off outside, of becoming self-centred, in order to survive. The very rich exchange of language and feeling is much harder in a small space – anger can be more damaging and frightening, frustration less easy to bear and yet easy to handle. It is far safer to watch the telly than to argue, far easier to go and wander outside than to ask for attention and find answers to questions. A mother overburdened with children is *less* able to cope with giving them adequate mothering in a small space than in a large one – how can she encourage water play, bricks, painting, reading, fantasy play, when she's exhausted, everyone is under feet and she has to get a meal ready on the top landing?

Nevertheless, the release from overcrowding does not solve the problem of the parents who do not know how to do it. Some parents, as we know, are themselves so deprived that they cannot give anything to their children except their own hatred and lack of self-esteem. Some families *do* break up, *do* have illnesses, sadnesses, death. The children of these families then, have, as well as the normal happy working-class cultural background to affect them, the potential of developing well or badly according to the actual degree of healthy parenting they receive which is common to *all* children. The three interactive factors, so closely interlocking it is often difficult to sort them out, must always be carefully appraised. What has the general environment done to this child? What has the *family* environment and, thirdly, what *is* this child of himself, potentially, what is his heredity, and his basic type, if that is the right word?

REFERENCES

1. *Patterns of Infant Care in an Urban Community*. John and Elizabeth Newsome. Penguin 1965.
2. *Birmingham Project for under fives*. No longer available.
3. *Education and Day Care for young children in need*. T. Blackstone. Bedford Square Press 1973. *Influences on Human Development (Illinois)*. Bronfen Briemer. Dryden Press 1972.
4. *The Delinquent Way of Life*. D. J. West and D. P. Farrington. Heinemann 1977.

CHAPTER 2

Some effects of deprivation

The low expectancies of socially deprived young people has, of course, frequently been described. It was quite remarkable to move from the group of boys I knew well to a new group of those who were early leavers, but who had *not* been selected by the Head to join my group, that is, who showed no particular behaviour difficulties and whose progress through the school had been pretty average. These boys would not have been in the main 'at risk' by the terms of our register and would probably not be known by the Care Committee Workers. I found that they had *far* higher aspirations. These boys, far from wanting to leave school and go direct into whatever job offered most money, were thoughtful of the future. They could accept the frustration of low paid jobs which offered some kind of training and could see the need to put off gratification of material needs till later. Most of them had fathers who encouraged this attitude. The fathers were not all 'white collar' workers by any means, some were labourers, but nearly all had been able, by encouragement and family 'conditioning', to offer their sons a level of self-esteem which prevented them from needing to act badly at school, encouraged learning as useful and hoped for a *better* future for the boy than they had had themselves.

At all levels their social circumstances were better than the other group: most had adequate housing, smaller families, and united parents. I do not want to imply the material wealth is all that important, but that it is useful in determining the likely future of a boy to look at his home and accept that the quality of the family regard for him will be a crucial factor in the development of self-esteem and of job aspirations.

The ordinary mother without giving a great deal of conscious thought to it offers her child, day in and day out, affection, regard, opportunities for exploration, discipline, criticism, and standards. She feeds the child the materials for him to develop self-esteem, inner control, adventurousness, a need to learn, an ability to move forward into new situations and show concern for other people. The father acts as a model with which the boy can identify, encouraging, accepting, demanding. The marriage that is stable and loving provides the child with a sense of trust and enables him to learn within his own home how to deal with relationships, how also to deal with frustration, anger, jealousy, despair and other negative feelings.

It is very hard for school-teachers to contend with the boy who has not had the privilege of ordinary family life for, of course, even by the age of five the situation may have become relatively unchangeable.

The child who comes from an emotionally poverty-stricken home will have obvious problems. He will not see the point of learning, partly because all early efforts to explore have been frustrated or put down, partly because nobody has cared for him sufficiently to give him the primary trust in himself and his environment. He will, however, because he is empty of the normal warm feelings incorporated from his parents have, along with a grave lack of self-esteem, a severe sense of emptiness and feelings of anger. In order to *feel* better, he will have to persuade himself that he is bigger, can have a greater effect on his environment, can 'show them' he exists. So he makes a noise, makes a nuisance of himself, swears, cusses and apparently despises everyone. The only way he can be rid of his anger is to lash out. So he becomes a bully, joins gangs, acts delinquently. I shall deal in more detail with all these symptoms in later chapters, but for the present would like to generalize upon them. The delinquent method of dealing with empty and angry feelings has, of course, no healthy resolution. If a boy 'rolls' a queer, he may get quite a lot of fun out of it at the time; if he takes a car and drives it he may also find it quite a lark. If he steals he may gain possessions, or acclaim from his mates; but in all these activities he is left at the end worse off than before. He may well end up in Juvenile Court, which is one end to the behaviour, but far more important he finds he does not feel better, but worse. He hates even more, feels even more empty, can find within the delinquent act no experience that increases his real stature or self-esteem because the acts are all based on negative concepts, in that the bad feelings are seen as outside the boy (i.e. the Queers, the Rich, the Blacks, etc.) and attacking these, or gaining materially does not therefore make the boy better. The only solution to his problem in the end is to learn to discover his own value and have trust in this, thus establishing a sense of responsibility to 'himself. After this value has been gained he can then relate to the world and see the validity of other people's needs, have a degree of empathy with them. If then he hates something or someone he can decide how to deal *with* this hate. If he hits out he takes responsibility for his feelings *about* it and any punishment he may get arising *from* it. So that the empty uncared for boy is not only unable to hold frustration, put off personal gratification for a greater aim, but can at no point *relate* effectively with another person. He has not identified with parents and he cannot *see* other people as real, only as in the way, or there to be exploited.

He sets a problem to others, of course, because initially no technique of handling seems effective. If one attempts to understand his predicament and show kindness and leniency he, because of his basic lack of trust, will take immediate advantage of it, seeing it as 'weakness' and having a catch in it, so that he will exploit the situation to the limit. The problem for him, of course, is that even if the real concern of the teacher is perceived, it may awaken such overpowering feelings of need that his only defence would be to deny and act offensively. On the other hand if one is punitive and excessively strict then the boy has the excuse himself to exercise his own hostility in retaliation, confirming him in this projection that 'they' are despicable and in fact that he is also, though he may not recognize it. His only salvation lies in gradually being helped to gain self-awareness while at the same time being placed in a position where he is never unfairly or excessively, but always effectively and steadily, held.

A secure, fairly highly disciplined environment where he is safe so that his hostility will *not* be destructive to himself or others can enable him, very gradually, to accept the respect others are offering him. By doing this he can eventually respect himself and them.

It may be that it is this ability on the part of institutions to hold and yet to care for the child that may have been lost. It is absolutely right, I would think, to condemn counter-hostility by staff, but it is just *as* right to condemn negative sweetness and permissiveness for the reasons stated.

If a child of about four years old can shout at a mother 'I hate you, I wish you were dead' he has already gained some inner control in that he can talk *about* his feelings knowing that he will be relieved by talking about them and also knowing

12

that the feelings themselves will not have the effect he so desperately fears – that the mother will die. So that expressing in words the terrible half-truth the child can then receive from the mother the reassurance that she realizes that at that point in time the child hates her, but that at the same time he is frightened of his hate and the effect it will have upon her. If the child is unable to speak, but in his fury kicks and scratches and screams, then the sensible parent has surely only one choice. She *holds* him, preventing him from hurting her, or *leaves* him until he feels better, but at all times is able to cope with the situation and restore love afterwards. The mother who herself loses her temper and hits back, or punishes the child for his *feelings*, the mother who coldly bites or scratches back 'to teach him how it feels' or the mother who wrings her hands and weeps or cajoles or threatens, cannot help the child to contain terrifying feelings and thereby gain maturity. I believe the situation is just the same in schools. So often deprived children have not reached the stage where they can *talk* about feelings, but can only act out hostility and so those in charge either cajole or counter-punish, that the child never learns the language of communication.

Therefore, at times of stress and severe unhappiness, anger or despair, the boy, rather than being able to ask for and obtain help, will make it extremely difficult for himself and his would-be helper by increasing his difficult behaviour and thus increasing the barrier between his upset feelings and the possibility of resolving them by verbal means. A number of adults use a similar mechanism. If I am hurt and sad I may well, instead of asking for help, make myself, to others, thoroughly disagreeable and block all their efforts to discover my malady, complaining bitterly that nobody cares a hoot what becomes of me and that I have no one who knows the meaning of friendship.

CHAPTER 3

Adolescence
The establishment of the 'self'

Adolescence is difficult, difficult for the adults as well as for the children. Parents in the main can cope with small children but do find larger ones very upsetting. The behaviour of the adolescent has a good deal in common with that of the toddler and in some ways the process is comparable.

The baby experiences its first real anxiety at the time that he recognizes his own separateness from and yet dependence upon his mother. His fury at not getting what he wants instantly (food and comfort) is only matched by his anxiety that it will never come and that he is absolutely helpless and alone. His relief when his mother rejoins with him is so exquisite that he develops love and, subsequently, trusts that she may not always be available but that she will be there.

Nevertheless she will often not be there when he wants her, so that fury will return and gradually, feeling more sense of the self but not yet aware of the world as separate from him, if she does not come he now is anxious lest his fury has annihilated her. He feels, in fact, alternately omnipotent and absolutely helpless. He gradually gains control over his feelings, but it takes longer to control his fantasies and children believe their fantasies to be so powerful that they actually can have powerful effects upon others and themselves.

A little girl attended Child Guidance Clinic. She was unable to settle, slept badly, was irritable, had temper tantrums and was a great problem to her parents. The psychiatrist could find no reason in the child to account for this at first, but on talking to her discovered that she had had a nanny of whom she was fond who had left. The child would say no more but obviously was very distressed. The family told the psychiatrist that they had had a rather strict nanny of whom the child was very fond. On her off-duty day nanny had gone out, got knocked down in the street and been killed. The parents had never told the child, thinking that she would be too upset but had said Nanny had gone on a long holiday and wouldn't be back for a good long time. When the psychiatrist told the child the truth, she burst into tears and then said how glad she was, because they had had a tiff before nanny went out and the remark had been made that 'Nannies didn't like naughty little girls like that and might go away and not return if little girls behaved badly'. The child had strongly believed that this was exactly what had happened. When nanny's death was explained she was so relieved not to have been rejected for her wickedness, but needed a good deal of support not to feel that in some way she had contributed to the death. After this she was well again and able to continue a normal childhood.

Adolescents have far more sense of omnipotence than we realize and, coupled with their very great anxiety about their own inadequacy, can cause themselves great anxiety. 'I couldn't tell my mum, it would kill her' could be translated as 'I've done something awful that I think will dreadfully upset mother. She might respond by being terribly angry with me, which I couldn't bear. On the other hand I terribly need comfort because I am alone and afraid. If I seek comfort this awful thing I've done will either destroy me, or will destroy my mother's love for me, or will destroy my mother, therefore I can't tell her.' The very fact the statement is made suggests firstly that the child has still a very strong attachment and need for her mother, secondly that she is moving away from the mother and trying to establish her own behaviour pattern but recognizes it might not be the same as her mother's (i.e. she sees them as separate) but at the same time she feels that any action of hers could have an over-whelming response in the other i.e. *'kill her'*.

The little child is very confused as to what is himself and what is 'other'. In some ways so is the adolescent. I want to deal later with the difficulties adolescents experience in separating their own problems from their parents' but I will give an example here. The deprived boy who puts all the blame on 'them' for his bad humour, is, in fact, not aware that the pain lies in him and not in the world. The girl who writes to me and says she is so lonely always and 'if only I could find a decent Youth Club . . . if only I went to a better school . . . if only my house and/or parents weren't so *awful*, all would be well' is, in fact, telling me quite often that she feels depressed but can't realize this, and sees the solution to it outside herself and not within.

The task of the adolescent assisted normally by parents, teachers

and friends, is to discover for himself the fact that the difficulties
do lie within. Sometimes this is impossible and further help has
to be given by counsellors, psychotherapists or other skilled aides.
We have seen how the deprived child may express empty and
angry feelings by delinquent behaviour, the more neurotic way
of dealing with this might be to show symptoms of apathy, tearfulness, lack of concentration and withdrawal.

The small child gradually becomes aware of his separateness
from the mother and from all the objects in the world and gains
trust by recognizing that objects are not in fact hostile, nor can
they be changed by hostile feelings on the part of the child,
and that people are supportive, warm and kindly and have their
own ways of behaviour independently. This separateness becomes
safe and yet dependency can be trusted and assured. The various
techniques of dealing with anxiety are established at a real level,
using mother and subsequently father, relatives, friends and
teachers for comfort and for pleasure; at fantasy level by getting
rid of anxiety in play, both verbal and non-verbal.

The adolescent has now finally to break the dependency ties
and establish independence and uses very much the same techniques, but one task he has which perhaps the toddler does *not*
is to develop the ability to think, act and conceptualize for himself,
even if this leads to decisions and beliefs that his parents do
not hold. the emerging awareness of the self is expressed firstly
in the growing Narcissism of the individual. The preening of
the young is, of course, mainly sexually orientated, but it does
carry within it an element of very healthy self-enquiry – 'What
do I look like, *feel* like? What clothes suit me? What hair-style?'

Thought also becomes rather narcissistic – the individual wants
to know *how* he feels, what his needs are, what his likes and
dislikes are, what his ideals and aspirations are. At first these
concepts are pretty cloudy and, in the very deprived child with
little sense of self, minimal. the sense of absolute longing and
hunger and the despairing sense of emptiness and fury is there,
but it cannot be expressed in understandable terms.

In order to establish the self the adolescent has several
techniques. The most familiar categories, I suppose, roughly fall
into the following groups:

(1) Family

'Here is my family; because it's my family I must fight free of

16

them. Because I trust them most, I dare to rebel chiefly against them, test their values. I therefore push as hard as I can against them. If they want me to have short hair, I grow it long, if they like classical music, careers, the Tory party, religion, I spurn them. Yet I love them and want them to love me. If they let me have all my differences, I feel lost because I *want* them to disagree in order to establish what I am, but if they push me *too* hard I get furious, or run away, or behave even more in a way they don't want. If they are utterly rigid I will burst from them, if they are very liberal they don't love me and don't care.'

In a study of alcoholism for example it was found that young people tended to drink too much if *either* their parents had been extremely opposed to drinking or had been totally uncaring as to whether the children drank or didn't, and especially if one parent had a bit of a drink problem themself. If families used alcohol in a social sense, taking it at home in moderation, then there was *far* less chance of the children becoming alcoholics. So *some* warlike situations between parents and children are a necessary part of growing up. A similar situation, of course, exists between children's teachers. I shall deal with the difficulties encountered by children, parents and teachers in more detail in later chapters.

(2) The Peer Group

Young people are extremely vulnerable. They have very little experience of independence so far, they have a very active fantasy life, are anxious concerning their concepts of themselves in relation to sexuality, ambition, and general self-esteem. They have to break from the childhood position but feel very often inadequate for the task. Partly because of their own anxieties they cannot always relate in depth to any one child. They may believe the other won't like them, may carry all sorts of false impressions of the other and certainly of themselves, but except in certain cases where their peer group is seen as frightening or unattainable, most adolescents gain great comfort from their loose associations with one another. Groups and gangs are very often far more fluid than is generally supposed, but nevertheless the peer group is of very great importance.

Sometimes the group is formed for a negative purpose – against another gang, to establish territorial rights, or as a way to relieve hostile feelings. A group setting out to 'rumble' the blacks, or Cyps, etc., sometimes within the group, even if it *is* set up for

17

negative reasons there is a core of mutual help, recognition and trust along with complex hierarchies, rules, uniforms and mystiques.

This is not the place to discuss the phenomena of gangs and it has been well established, but there is no doubt that the gang offers a sense of strength, real as well as fantasy, to the adolescent.

One kind of loose association or gang is based upon group assumption of hostility, not against rival peer groups, but against real or imagined wrongs in society. In these groups there is generally an ideology expressed and an effort either to opt out of a society seen as bad or to change a society seen as bad. In this situation there might be, at least initially, considerable conceptualizing concerning the meaning of the group. A group language, uniform, mystique would also be developed but there would be some common purpose or aim. Boy Scouts and Girl Guides are, I suppose one example of this though, being *adult* conceived they could only be adhered to while the individuals *within* the group agreed to the aims formulated by the adults responsible for the rules. Some youth clubs are similar and so, in some ways, are almost all schools. The genuine groups I was describing would include those self-generating which are seen so clearly in the 'hippie' movement, the various drug cultures, some of the student organizations, squatting groups, and a few revolutionary groups.

The drug problem I will also deal with later, but the groups which identify themselves as being for the purpose of offering something *good* within them as well as opting out of a 'bad' society have a good deal to commend them to young people. Here the young can feel they can belong, have a private language and agree in total love. Here they can express their need to oppose society and their parents' wishes and here, in theory, they can 'extend their experience' by the intake of certain chemicals which enhance perception, increase feelings of kindliness and theoretically make the individual a better and different person. The drug culture expressed like this could represent to the young person not ready yet to be totally independent and feeling exposed, young, lonely, unsure, all the ingredients of happiness and security.

(3) Society

The adolescent, in looking outwards at society can find ways

18

of finding an identity. The evaluation of all things seen and heard and felt, including painting, music, dancing and reading; the appraisal of the structures and aims of societies, of politics, social groupings and religions are all brought to bear in testing concepts, ideals and pleasures. The young person also tests by practical experience *himself* in relation to this. Can *he* paint, draw, dance, make music, make poetry? Can *he*, involved in religion or politics, organize for change, can he train himself for excellence in sport? A frustrated human (and all humans are frustrated from the moment of birth in that they can never have *all the time* what they want, nor do, nor be, what they want) can allay his frustration in several ways. If I want to climb a mountain I discover that I need, among other things, training, good muscles, good balance, freedom from annihilating fear, some food, the right clothes, a map and an ability to contain discomfort. It may all be worth it if the goal is sufficiently important. On the other hand it may be that I desperately want to get to the top of the mountain but just don't believe I ever could. It might be I was right (I know I could never climb Mont Blanc, let alone Annapurna) so that even if I wanted to I would have to *accept* the frustration of looking at it but never reaching it. It might be that it *was* attainable, but that I felt so hopeless about my own ability to achieve what I wanted that I would never even try. If that was so I would almost certainly finish up by being very depressed and angry. I might blame my lack of money for clothes, or my 'heart' or those stupid people who wouldn't let me go, or the weather, but whichever I blamed, my frustration would remain.

I might, on the other hand, rush out of the house without decent clothes and with no map or food and tear up the mountain full tilt, jeering at everyone else until I either fell down a cliff, got caught in a snow storm or got lost.

All these techniques are shown by different individuals at different times.

A school child might hate school, yet he might very much want to achieve some goal that could only be attained *at* school. At one level, perhaps an exam, at a more real and personal level, an understanding of a problem. This frustration might make it necessary to accept very unpleasant situations, very boring learning processes, very many rejections or sneering by other people, but if his sense of trust in *himself* and his ability to accept the guidance of others, then with a high enough frustration level, he will accept all the difficulties as an essential part of reaching the goal. As a moderately happy and intelligent child, brought up in a family that enjoyed learning and encouraged skills, that took for granted 'careers', that also believed profoundly in hard work and study for its own sake in order to achieve an eventual heaven and a 'good character', I was thrust as well as driven by my own as well as their expectations of me. It never entered my head *not* to study. In fact, probably because I was the most fearful prig, the other girls at school didn't like me and I must confess that I adored not only doing well and 'coming top' but also the work for its own sake. This enjoyment of work failed me dismally at college for all sorts of reasons, but it was and is a pretty commonplace description of an average middle-class child.

If I had been slightly more oppressed by my view of myself in relation to my family, school-mates and God, I might, and many, many children alas do, have pinned *all* my anxieties upon study itself. I might have worried and fretted desperately, pursuing study as an ever disappearing pot of gold at the end of some far distant rainbow, panting, urgent, sleepless. I saw a boy recently who produced for me 78 rules by which he could conduct his life in order to pass his exams. I will deal with his sort of problem in a separate chapter, but here I want to exemplify the typical neurotic response to anxiety caused by external, family and internal problems at adolescence. The response that makes it imperative for the child (and the adult, too, as a matter of fact) to attach his problem to the wrong cause and, like a dog endlessly seeking for a non-existent bone, exhaust himself by his own anxiety. The solution to the boy's problem was *not* to work harder and harder, but to pull back from work, offer himself a respite in order to allow the *real* problem sufficient time to well up and show itself. *Then* the task of dealing with it becomes possible and eventually no doubt the exams get taken.

(He reminds me of adult patients who get so fretted about sleeplessness that they can't sleep; no amount of sleeping tablets cure the problem because the *real* problem is not looked at, and it is the *real* problem that is causing the lack of sleep. Sometimes it's even simpler, in that the individual may not actually need much sleep and those who say, and so many of them do, but Doctor, I still *wake* tired are not telling us they haven't had enough sleep *per se*, but that they are so overwrought

20

from *some other cause* that sleep will not cure it, nor even be given a chance.)

Some children, as we well know, have such little self-esteem, that their ability to see a solution to frustration in terms of eduction are minimal. If you can't read it is necessary firstly to *mind* that you cannot, to find it *awkward*. Secondly you must trust yourself sufficiently, acknowledge that it is worth while to try to learn, and thirdly you must trust someone enough to let them teach you. Alas, there are a considerable number of children where *none* of the criteria exist.

It is surprisingly easy to get through present-day life with very little reading ability. The radio talks to you, the television gives you pictures, your friends chatter and *do*, i.e. act. You can learn the workings of a motorbike without reading, you can watch football without reading, you can chat up a bird – but what you can't do is find out things for yourself other than at a practical level. Many boys have been ashamed not to be able to write love letters to their girls, though telephones have, I suppose, made it easier. But it's very understadable that a boy or girl could devalue schooling utterly if they were in a position in which learning, culture, communication were seen not only as useless but as a mockery.

If a family does not have expectations of their children, loves them vaguely but is not involved with them, if in that family the written word is not used much, and even the spoken word is not other than for day-to-day speech, if the child has no drive from within his family to 'better himself' and not much *self* esteem, then any frustration he has is not directed towards his agonising inability to *know* enough, but toward a vague apprehension that he wants to 'get' them, or a passive retreat into inactivity. What, after all, is the use of learning if it's all going to be the same in the end?

Finally, if the child, both by cultural patterning and by experience, finds that 'they' – the teachers – despise him, 'put him down' or offer him totally irrelevant material as schooling, no wonder a total block against it occurs.

It is heartrending for eager and compassionate teachers to be faced with a mulish, rejecting and totally uninterested mob of apparent savages. No amount of caring, or trying seems to break the enormous barrier between teacher and pupil, and yet it can be done. What seems to them absurd is that the primary school child really does seem to *live* at school, whereas the secondary school child, after the first year or so, seems to drop out of the whole system, becoming either physically or emotionally far away and immune. I am not writing a book on school as an institution, but a book on counselling, but it seems important to point out at times the need to clarify the problem of children at school in this way. So that with under-achieving children, as in all situations where they do not live up to our expectation, we have to say – where is the fault? Is it the school *system*? Can we modify the institution and the curriculum? Is it the teaching or the teachers? Do they offer material in a relevant manner? Do they *listen* enough as well as talk, do they *respect* the child? We have to look at what society is telling the child about school and about himself. Is society evading the institution of school, publicly acclaiming it, but privately deriding it? Do books, magazines, radio, television in fact subtlely offer such different prizes that school values seem absurd? Does our society, while publicly offering freedom of choice in careers and jobs in fact, by its very structure, make certain that the class distinctions stay pretty well as they always have? Doctors' children become doctors, professional people's children more often appear in grammar schools, Army officers' children at Sandhurst. A few 'working-class' children make the grade. Why is this? Is it as a result of genetic inheritance, family expectation, or society's unspoken social closed doors?

What do parents do or not do to modify childhood expectations and attitude to school? It's quite obvious when sitting in Juvenile Court that although many parents are warned that their children don't go to school, among them are a high number who aren't at all surprised, and who can blame them if they hated school themselves, and a smaller number who would agree heartily with the child or positively encourage him in his non-attendance? So that in discussing childhood aspiration we *have* to look at the reality of the environment to which he has been exposed – personal, family and social.

And what in effect *do* we want for our children? We talk vaguely about happiness, but by that do we really mean material possessions? We talk about kindness and fairness, but to be kind you have to have a sufferer, and aren't we often only too ready to find suffering in order that we ourselves feel better?

Society *is* us and represents a common viewpoint. It's an odd society, it offers television sets, washing machines, pollution, extraordinarily delicate surgery, research, frightful neglect of the old, the insane and the stupid; it offers Rolls-Royces and holidays on the Costa Brava and has the highest prison population for a long time. Prisoners who have learnt to want washing machines and holidays but have set about it the wrong way. Subnormal and mentally ill people who found the system too difficult to play. The public gardens are filling up with alcoholics and the banks with money – what on earth does an adolescent make of it all?

CHAPTER 4

Adolescence
Some difficulties: Loneliness, Sexuality, Drugs

It's quite difficult to describe the adolescent because, of course, he is as diverse as is the adult, child or ancient, but I think there are enough common factors to enable us to see him as, for the purpose of this book, separate from adults and children.

The adolescent, as already stated, has little sense of the self. He or she is growing fast both physically and intellectually. His emotional life is lurching into powerful and exquisite situations. If you are not very sure of yourself and the world you inhabit, one relief is to live in fantasy. The fantasies of adolescence are of enormous importance. They can be a relief and they can be a great burden and hopefully they can lead the child into concepts through processes, ideologies and self knowledge by experience.

I have already discussed the need of adolescents to gain a sense of reality by pushing hard at parents and teachers and by joining with peer groups. I would like briefly to discuss the difficulties they have in relating to the unknown self and to other people.

Loneliness

I have already shown how very lonely some young people can feel and how one technique they have is to assume that the solution lies outside themselves. If a girl says she's lonely, she is probably also saying she feels unloved, different and excluded. In fact she really – though it's hard to help her see this – is feeling (and I hate the word but have to use it here) alienated from herself. It is, of course, so easy to see a problem as away from you and not belonging to you.

Nicola was a fairly large, but pretty girl. She was doing quite badly at school. She could scarcely read and although not really stupid, was seen by teachers, children, her parents and herself as a bit of a dunce.

The school had recognised her learning problem and had given her remedial teaching, though now she was struggling in an ordinary class as it was felt she could manage.

The school doctor knew she was very unhappy and was encouraging her to slim, so that she would not feel so different from the other children.

The mother was trying to help by encouraging dieting (though this was difficult as she herself found food a great compensation for unhappiness and her other children were greedy people). The mother also worried a good deal as she felt her daughter had reacted very badly to various family crises in the past which accounted for her present difficulty. Indeed the child had received some Child Guidance treatment years ago when she took a dislike to school in her junior years.

Nicola was friendly and talkative. She was terrified of school and very lonely. She said all the other children turned away when she came into the room, that no one would sit next to her, that they called her names, that the teachers were horrid to her, that she was worried about her mother's health, jealous of her brothers, that the father was useless and her home untidy and a mess.

There is no doubt Nicola has a problem. Firstly, she not only vaguely dislikes school but is really frightened of it. Secondly, she finds learning very hard. Thirdly she *is* overweight and *is* a compulsive eater and fourthly she *is* rather unpopular.

Each symptom separately does not necessarily constitute a problem, but together it adds up, and how can it be dealt with? Nicola is fifteen; she is, one can assume, at that stage of adolescence when she feels isolated and alone and unsure of herself. She is in a vicious circle because, being naturally unsure but emotionally extra confused and fat, she can always achieve what she most dreads, the external realization of how awful she is. She *is* fat, she *can't* read, the girls *don't* like her (and though she can't see this yet, she is continuing to keep this pattern going). She continues to eat, continues to be separate and continues to have work problems.

Now in normal adolescence the fantasies which we *fear*, because we want good things for ourselves, are hopefully displaced, so that we can put ourselves into a position where we can remove our own barriers. Ann, another girl, was also miserable at school. She loathed the high expectation, had frightful quarrels with her father, was rude and offensive to her mother and repeated over and over that if she could only find a youth club and leave that school all would be well. I saw her fairly regularly and, by taking the school problem seriously, gained her trust so that we could discuss her loneliness. It was not simple because there were parent expectations also to deal with, but by seeing the parents and helping them to accept Ann as she felt she was (i.e. not particularly academic), she was able to enjoy her new school immensely, make a number of friends and join various youth clubs. Ann was not in fact as simple a proposition as all that, but she was far enough along the road of adolescence to be helped to test the reality of some of her anxieties and to trust the helping hand of the adults involved. She was not, in fact, unhappy because she couldn't have friends or hated school so much as because she was frustrated in her search for the self by her parents' ambition on her behalf. Nicola, however, is stuck much deeper in her problem and illustrates more clearly the difficulties inherent in counselling of this age group. Ann *was* confused, but could eventually look at this confusion and sort out some of the strands. Nicola can't. The reason lies partly in maturation, partly in psychopathology. Ann could step aside from her parents just enough to stand up for herself (and she gave them both a pretty bad time). Nicola can't and there are two interlocking reasons for this: one lies in herself, that she is still very much a baby, and very much needs her parents and the other is her mother, who is emotionally very anxious and sad and needs her daughter (as her daughter vaguely realizes) to stay dependent, so that mother and child are still caught up in a tight relationship.

Nicola can't get thinner partly because food represents love and warmth, partly because her mother desperately needs to *give* her food, neither can she gain independence sufficiently to join children of her own age because she has to remain 'small'. So that her 'feeling' she is different and the children's recognition of this, is correct. The same problem, of course, occurs in highly intelligent children. Andrew felt just as lonely at school – was absolutely certain that . . . if only the boys liked him, he could find a club, etc., etc. In fact the boys might well not like him, I don't know, but he *felt* different and felt alone. The reality and the fantasy tend to merge and eventually the fears are banished by the ability to move into new situations because one has sufficient need to achieve what one wants (compassion) to quell the assumption one can't do it.

One of the difficulties of early adolescence lies in the inability to see other people as they really are. We have touched on this before, but I think we need to look at it again now. Adults frequently don't grow out of this themselves, but hopefully they are better at it – we all, to some extent, make assumptions about other people ranging from 'knowing the black man's . . . Jew's . . . women's . . . character' to having notions in relation to how other people are responding to us which modify our responses and can become absolutely ludicrous; this happens a good deal at work, in marriage and in all relationships, both in groups (politics is a fine example) and individually. But adolescents are even less able to stay, as it were, behind their own skins than we.

Two sets of problems can arise from this. Firstly the child can be so totally identified with family that he cannot see himself as separate (and Nicola is an example) and secondly, when he does try to establish one-to-one relationships he may at first make an awful hash of it.

Sexuality

The drive towards achievement and job satisfaction and the sense of self esteem it may offer is usually considered the major force in the struggle for maturity.

The drive towards happiness, or joy, seems to me to be more encompassing and profound. Of *course* I prefer warmth to coldness, enough good food to hunger, and love rather than rejection. I feel happy and alive in preference to feeling dreary and depressed (unless I'm a masochistic prig, in which case I get some gain from feeling good about feeling bad). The marvellous tender experiences of suckling a baby, sniffing an early primrose on a lovely sunny March morning, the incredible assault upon the ears of a particular moment in a piece of music, the sweet melody of a poem, how can we not see these experiences as good, but the overwhelming longing for the touch on the skin, the kiss and the embrace, the extraordinary upsurge of sexual joy, the free flow of caring, loving and erotic pleasure is still hidden away by most adults in a pretence it doesn't happen or isn't very nice, or is pretty low. Adolescents are experiencing *all* these feelings and sometimes they are very alarming. Relief from the overwhelming upsurge can be obtained sometimes by creative activity – music, drama, dancing, painting, walking, playing games of skill, developing fierce ideological concepts. The need for caring can be expressed partially by good works and religion but the passionate feelings tend to stay all the same. Adolescents escape from some of their anxiety by withdrawal into a private solitary world, a world where the tumult can be assuaged in dreams. Parents have no place in this world, nor do other adults. It is so intensely private, perhaps shameful, often very fragile, and the adolescent can put up extremely strong defences against invasion; at the same time, however, because it is all so overwhelming, they feel desperately lonely and in need of help and resent the fact that their parents/teachers don't help, don't understand. This dual need to keep precious and private and yet to find comfort and help makes it difficult for child and adult. The alternating need for independence (privacy) and dependence (sharing) is absolutely characteristic and establishes the pattern where adults have to accept that they can never be right.

If a child has had a pretty normal upbringing, if for example, she has experienced the constancy of two parents' affection for her and for each other and if she has been given the privilege of enjoying her body and understanding about sexuality, then the sexual feelings, muddled and confused as they must be, can gradually be understood and welcomed.

At first boys and girls *have* to be 'self' centred. It is a time when the puzzle is to find out *what* he feels, *what* he is, the boy cannot see other people as real and valuable. For one thing he is too busy unravelling the connecting threads between himself and his parents, for another he is still very confused about his own value and the value of his sexuality. Boys practically all masturbate, a smaller proportion of girls do. The fact of masturbation is still, alas, wrapped in taboos and misapprehensions so that many boys and girls feel very guilty and are at the mercy of old wives' tales. I think the guilt is not *all* to do with social inacceptance, but stems also from anxiety in the individual himself concerning the goodness or badness of his *own* sexuality, his ability to accept his need for pleasure and his anxiety about potency. Nevertheless society's taboos reinforce this. At the beginning of adult sexual life relationships do not have a part to play. Boys may collaborate with one another in masturbatory activities, but there is no real sexual relationship present.

Boys quite sensibly perhaps move from masturbation into wanting something better. The act of intercourse is not only more pleasurable, but also offers a very real goal of manhood achieved and a personal status and relief from anxieties over impotence. The girl involved will frequently not be seen as a person, only as an object of pleasure. Normally the ability to care for the partner, the wish to please her, to wish to give as well as receive, in fact the experience of affection and love will follow fairly quickly so that heterosexual attachment rather than activity is achieved. The relief of this can be great, because now the man can utilize all his good feelings in the development of a close and joyful friendship which includes sex but is not exclusively *for* sex.

At the time of 'self' centredness it is unlikely that a boy would give much to the girl (except, alas, a baby) in that he would be so busy working through his own feelings he could not reach out to hers, so that responsibility for the girl would not probably enter his head. If he really did hold her in esteem for herself then he would want her to be willing and joyful, and would want to please her as well as himself.

The common attitude toward boys is that they are self-seeking, wanting instant gratification without caring for the other, unwilling to take responsibility for the other; that they brag, are loud-mouthed, rude and aggressive.

In talking with the school group and with heterosexual groups in Youth Clubs I think the truth lies at some distance from this. Boys are to a greater or lesser extent depending upon personality and environment, anxious about sexuality but do also need pleasure now, this instant. They do find girls strange and embarrassing. They develop various techniques to enable them to feel better.

They brag, firstly, with one another and secondly to girls. They find that by pretending a competence they don't feel they can win some self respect by achieving respect from others. They use girls as objects, partly because they genuinely are not ready yet to make relationships, partly because by denying the reality of the girl's feelings they can free themselves of anxiety. They therefore will go all out to get a girl, but will make assumptions that if they achieve their aim it's because the girl wanted it, which

29

is the equivalent of saying she is a 'slag'. So any girl 'having it off' with them is a baddie. Paradoxically, any girl refusing them becomes a challenge, but the challenge is too much at first and the attempt becomes not worth the effort. Later it may be that respect for the girl can emerge.

They also, to the misery of the girls, have another habit; if they take a girl out they can reach a level of quite deep intimacy, but if the next day they see her while in the company of their male friends they may cut her dead. The girls will show off to one another that they have been out with a boy, the boys will feel ashamed. They must appear careless and uninterested to their mates and confess to being pretty shy anyway, as though having gone out with a girl they don't know what to do next.

In a book about boys in East London, the shame experienced by boys in first developing heterosexual attachment and moving away from the gang is very clearly expressed. the gentle and sentimental feelings of affection can be very deeply hidden and can produce great conflict. I think that this is nothing like so obvious in the more middle-class boys who have been enabled by parents to express gentle feelings throughout their childhood.

Boys, perhaps even more than girls, deal with their ambivalent sexual feelings by denial of the possible goodness of love. One method of dealing with anxiety is to laugh it off. The endless series of defaecatory and sexual jokes which are a part of childhood, adolescence and indeed adulthood, are expressions of the anxiety that we all feel about the goodness or badness of our bodily functions and our ability to control them. The boys in the club and at the school assaulted me at first with loud laughs, rude words, seductive statements and questions which superficially were absurd and extremely provocative, but because I accepted that this behaviour acted as a cloak to hide very real anxiety the language gradually became less provocative and the questions better defined. This is not a book on sex education, so I shall say no more on this topic, but I am quite sure that in common with all humanity, the adolescent boys wanted to find a way to be loving and to have a good marriage, giving their wives the affection they could recognize their mothers so often lacked.

Some boys are more aware of their real anxieties and, if given the opportunity, can discuss them with a trusted individual. Boys do have masturbation anxiety, they do have worries about potency. Sometimes they approach a doctor complaining of tiredness or back ache, sometimes they complain of acne, sometimes that their penis may be the wrong size or shape. The symptom they present depends upon how nearly they can allow themselves to look at the truth about themselves, but any counsellor or doctor who attacks the symptom without giving the boy the chance to reveal his hidden worries is not really helping the child.

The anxiety about homosexual feelings is very real. Public school boys may be conditioned to accept that as well as using one another for sexual play (without affection) they may in fact become very fond of another boy or a male teacher. In working-class families, I think this normal state of affairs may not be so well accepted. The fantasies (particularly during masturbation) may be powerfully homosexual and the fears concomitantly terrifying. Adherence to a formal gang structure, one that has common aims and vows of allegiance and leadership, may assuage some of the anxieties, but nevertheless we must, I think, accept that a number of boys are very scared of this phase of their life and worry lest it becomes permanent. One meets with exactly the same problem in girls.

I know a girl who, in fact, almost certainly will continue to be homosexual for a time at least, who fell in love with a teacher. At first she dreamed the days away thinking up stories where the two of them were together. Nothing overtly sexual took place so that the fantasies relieved her feelings considerably. Gradually, however, as the reality became clearer and the affection deepened the girl became terrified. She had had an extremely disturbed childhood and was able to recall that whenever gentle feelings were experienced she always fled from them either by turning her back or by attacking whoever was showing concern for her. Faced with the teacher she loved, she panicked. At first she abused her verbally, but this did not seem to help. The teacher was still kindly and friendly. In despair, she attacked the teacher, punched her, locked her in a cupboard. She was, of course, expelled from school. Eventually she made another attachment and this time was enabled to understand more clearly what was happening and to talk the whole problem through with the person involved.

I mention this because I think we must recognize that children, dealing with fear and anxiety, can act in various ways; they can act *out* in hostility, bragging and aggression or they can turn inwards with passivity, depression or other symptoms. Sometimes the acting out is in the form of denial. Some promiscuous boys and girls are in fact attempting to stave off fears of homosexuality by their frantic heterosexual encounters.

Girls

The response of girls to adolescence is, of course, just as varied as is that of boys. The girl can only learn the reality of her own feelings by experience and is also at the mercy of the various external factors, social and cultural, which modify her ability to see herself as she really is. Just as the boy is conditioned by his town, street, class and parental expectation, so, too, is the girl. I have already mentioned the attitudes of a group of girls in a Youth Club toward marriage, career and boyfriends, an attitude that expresses very clearly their closeness to family expectation and identification with them and also shows a sad lack of adventurousness and self-esteem. It is fashionable at present to propose that girls are placed in a 'second rate' position from the moment of birth by their family and the society in which they find themselves, and there is no doubt that there is a good deal of conditioning going on. Girls *are* encouraged to wear pink, play with dolls, cook, sew, be gentle and kind to other children and to look to a safe marriage as a goal. Boys *are* encouraged to wear blue, be lively, noisy and dirty, play with cars and seek physical adventure, before ultimately achieving a well-paid job, a house, a wife and one or two children. But the influence of family and society (including school) does not so much change the gender orientation as express in perhaps over emphatic terms a difference which is already there.

I have no doubt, and study after study has shown, that girls and boys from birth, exhibit differing behaviour and interests. One study has shown that a new-born *girl* will make far more mouth movements than a boy and that the boy will make more limb movements. The mother, however, will also modify her responses. She will fondle the boy's limbs more and cuddle the girl less. Already the parent and the child are forging a relationship which encourages a normal difference to emerge more strongly.

If boys and girls are given a free range of play materials they will *both* seek, at appropriate ages, common play material, but the time the boys spend upon cars, engines, climbing, etc., will be longer than the girls and girls will spend longer on dolls and 'caring' games.

Sex Differences | Roles | Play

I mention this because it seems to me that it is so easy for people to make assumptions about girls and boys based upon fallacies and prejudice, assumptions upon which can be erected beautiful concepts of education, urgent revolutionary messages and sometimes very funny literature, but perhaps, as there could not be a child brought up *without* an external environment, *nor* without a basic gender (except on rare occasions of hermaphroditism) or a basic genetic inheritance, then one must be aware of the importance of all influences. From the latter, the most important influence upon gender identification and aspiration lies within the family. The attitude of father and mother to their own and each other's identity will modify fundamentally that of the child. In later chapters, when dealing with specific problems of adolescence I shall come back to this. At present I wish to highlight some of the facets which troubled adolescent girls present.

In general girls are more inhibited than boys, their sexual feelings tend to be far more diffuse. It is less common for them to masturbate and for them to have precise sexual dreams and fantasies. If you talk to girls about sex, they nearly always link it with love and settling down (nesting). Biologically this is obviously very sound as the boy has to move toward the girl and she has simply to be receptive and able to provide a place for the baby to thrive.

Initially they are frightened. They talk a good deal about abnormality and pain, both within the sexual act and during labour. They also tend to orient their feelings far less toward direct personal enjoyment and more toward the giving of love and pleasure to the other.

In a survey in Sweden some years ago, upon asking girls and boys their response to first intercourse the girls were more likely to be a bit ashamed, the boys absolutely delighted.

The girl expresses her sexual development more in terms of vague yearnings and sentimental attitudes towards love and babies. She reads far more love stories and is less interested in pornography. In fact whereas sexual literature excites the boy, it often frightens the girl. It may be that part of this belongs to the literature and is not inherent in the girl. A good deal of sexual literature offers a picture of tremendous aggression on the part of the male and sometimes the female, so that the woman is seen as either submitting to fierce attack on herself, or herself as the attacker. This may suit the male fantasy, but it offers the average girl a reinforcement of her two anxieties: the first that sex will tear her, open her, change her, bruise her or hurt her; the second that if she clearly enjoys it she may have to acknowledge aggressive drives for personal satisfaction and for control of the other.

The girl will be very preoccupied with her appearance. She will long to look nice, be like the others, have a good figure, wear pretty clothes, not, perhaps as the boy does, in order to gain group acceptance or in order to call attention to himself as a male, but in order to disprove her anxieties about her own unattractiveness and unloveableness. I don't want to make too much of this, because both sexes are narcissistic, and in both sexes there are mixed feelings about appearance and worthiness, but I think girls are more inclined to want to please than to hurt. Anxieties about periods, acne, sweating, greasy hair – all present themselves and I suppose are the girl's defence against fears concerning femininity. Many girls complain about periods and although many of them genuinely have bad periods, yet a high proportion are suffering not because of a pathological process but because of a psychosomatic situation attached to fantasies concerning periods, sexuality and womanhood.

Although the boy suffers a good deal from the rapid and sudden change in his physical appearance and his biological drives, he does not have quite the same problem as does the girl. The hormonal level, triggered off at puberty, stays roughly the same from week to week and from year to year. The girl, however, experiences something different. Marie Stopes wrote in her early and, at the time, very shocking books on sex and marriage, that women fluctuate in their sexual desires in relation to their periods; it has since been shown by many workers that not only does sexual desire but also mood and sense of well being fluctuate. It is commonplace now to hear about premenstrual tension and premenstrual depression. It has been demonstrated that there are more suicides, more street accidents, and more school behaviour problems in the premenstrual phase of girls' and women's lives. Teachers are more strict and punitive and less able to contain frustration and girls are the same. The effect of the oral contraceptive can reinforce or remove this cyclic mood swing and, of course, so does the menopause. The adolescent girl therefore has to contend with an *overall* change in mood and feelings as well as with a cyclic change. She is therefore much more likely to draw attention to herself in class by her alternating moodiness and enthusiasm, pigheadedness, aggressiveness, solitariness and depression. It is often therefore more difficult to assess in a given child whether she really *is* a problem or *has* a problem.

The girl's response to sexuality therefore may be less direct than that of the boy. She has something to preserve, he something to achieve. The pressures of society, peer group and individual male and female are, however, now undergoing a vast change. To take them in order. It is now not necessarily 'the best' to stay a virgin until marriage. The effectiveness of contraceptive methods can prevent pregnancy. Moral value systems are changing: whereas in the past our society, at least overtly, established quite clearly that sex before marriage was wrong and quoted chapter and verse to prove it, nowadays these systems have been to a great extent demolished, so that now the tendency is to look inward more at individual morality rather than outward toward a general established doctrine. Sex is now (and again, at least overtly) seen as good and a part of loving, indeed as a very important part of loving, whereas in the past I think it indubitably was seen as bad, or at least dangerous if it 'got out of hand'. Very many young people believe that sex before marriage is good, not only enjoyable, but valuable as one way of deepening and strengthening relationships. But our society in, one must say, it's least healthy aspect, has picked upon sexuality as one of the best sales gimmicks of the century. Practically every substance advertised for sale to the young is linked to a sexual theme. Beer, petrol, cigarettes, chocolates, coffee, clothes, radios, the list is endless. Most books, short stories and comic series play upon the sexual theme. Why not? It sells the product and it also, of course, plays upon the anxieties and fantasies of the public. It's all right to say sex is good, etc., etc., but a very high proportion of young and not so young people are anxious still about their feelings. In the name of freedom, in fact a good deal in literature actually increases fears rather than diminishes them.

Girls, therefore, are offered very contradictory messages about sex. On the face of it it's good, it's modern, it's OK, but at a deeper level it's aggresive, dirty and bad. The peer group, the group of young people of the same age, is an odd phenomenon. In some ways it seems a unified whole, expressing the general feelings and attitudes of the young, used as a refuge by them from adults, used as a battlefront by them against adults, yet what *is* this group? It's a collection of young people each of whom is feeling isolated, vulnerable and unsure, but each of whom may well see *other* members of it as happy, secure, and belonging to one another. The effect of this non-cohesiveness of an apparently cohesive group is to force the insecure to attempt to achieve what she sees as the group ideology. She must gain status by copying even if she copies a myth. So she behaves as she would expect others to behave (at present this behaviour seems to be blank indifference, rudeness and total withdrawal from communication with other age groups).

Having sex now becomes not a matter of shame, but for the gaining of status.

A young girl, therefore, might well have sex not because she really wants it, or likes the boy, but because she needs to feel like the others.

In the struggle to achieve adulthood she also has to establish herself as separate from her parents. If the parents say sex is wrong then the girl may rebelliously use sex as her weapon against the parents. She may go to all-night parties, because promiscuous girls get to know the 'wrong sort of boys' in an effort to test the parents. I have already discussed this problem in relation to other kinds of behaviour, but to some parents this is the worst possible thing to happen. Very strict and rather uncaring parents may both have difficulties with teenage daughters. The one because the child finds it essential to burst through her chains, the other because she is desperately seeking limits and can't find them (and, also, and I'll come back to this, that she feels so unloved she looks for love wherever she can find it). Nearly all teenagers battle with their parents, and a number do so at this point, probably because there is such an obvious generation gap in attitudes toward sex.

Children sometimes have a good deal of difficulty because if they love and respect their parents they may have to find themselves in the position of making a choice at variance with their parents wishes. They would recognize the pain it caused the parents and yet feel it necessary in the light of their own conviction. Some parents can accept the fact that their children are good, kind and loving people, and yet make decisions upon moral behaviour at variance with their own; others cannot.

But some parents do make it difficult for themselves and for their daughters. Parents often find it very hard to believe that their children are growing up and able to take responsibility for their own lives; a proportion, I think, are themselves unhappy or dissatisfied and cannot bear to believe their children are growing away from them which is even more painful if the child appears to enjoy sexual freedom, when the mother was never allowed to have this freedom before marriage and unable to within marriage. It must be very difficult for a woman frustrated by her own inhibitions to accept the freedom of her children's lives.

Normal young people, then, gradually learn to decide for themselves how to deal with sexual feelings, whether to use sex as part of a relationship before marriage and what sex means to them as a joy in itself. But not all young people are able at first, anyway, to do this and are therefore pushed, as we have seen, by forces outside themselves into an activity for which they are unready or which they use as a weapon against authority or parent.

The individual girl is also struggling with her internal feelings of good and bad, loveableness and need for gratification. If she has had a moderately loving and peaceful home she gets through early adolescence without too many mistakes and finds herself involved at an appropriate time with decisions she can handle. If, however, she has had a very empty and unloved childhood, a series of catastrophes which involved loss of parents for one reason or another, her self esteem will be low and her hostility high. She may then be unable to make a good relationship because there is so little of herself but she will be unable to refuse any request by a boy for sex. At one level she will gain a little by seeing herself as being wanted and being able to give the boy a part of herself, which is good, but once the boy has had her, he will despise her and make her feel worse, so that instead of gaining by the experience she will lose. This repeats her previous experience of never trusting anybody because they have never stayed with her and her anger and pain will therefore remain, gradually she will reach toward some activity such as prostitution where her hatred for men can be played out endlessly, or toward a slightly more hopeful expression of need, getting pregnant with it's offer of 'something to love'.

Girls who embark upon an active sexual life at an early stage of adolescence are not necessarily sick or damaged. We do not label boys as sick if they do – we accept that 'boys will be boys'. In some cultures, it has been accepted that 'girls will also be girls' but usually that culture was of a kind where the rather promiscuous sexual activity seemed to occur in a young population who were relatively infertile or where the family grouping was such that occasional pregnancies were acknowledged and assimilated. In our culture this is, by and large, not the case. Young girls become fertile very young and a large proportion of families in Great Britain cannot assimilate its illegitimate children. With the development of effective contraception, this has, at least potentially, changed but even so I think it is difficult for adults to accept the normality of sex for girls without attachment and love. It may be that girls will gradually become in behaviour more like boys, free to experience sexuality at first without ties, and gradually to develop the need for deeper and longer lasting relationships.

But among our young people there obviously are some who are not in fact ready, if that's the right term. Some are what I will call 'pseudo-adult' they have skipped from childhood to a mask of adulthood without the necessary experience of adolescence – that experience which involves some homosexual feelings, a good deal of narcissism and swings of mood between childishness and adulthood. These young people, for some reason, cannot allow themselves the value of adolescence and can only see the adult world as offering a goal without any benefits for them.

Some are struggling with feelings of emptiness or deprivation, some with very complex involvement in a parental and family situation. Some are at war with their family either for personal reasons or mixed with cultural differences between home and school.

There is a sad and very real lack of knowledge about sex among young people. If, as I think we must agree is the case, each individual has to be responsible for his own decisions and actions, then it is the responsibility of adults to offer appropriate information and guidance so that the young person can decide effectively. Therefore sex education should be given to all children and this should include information concerning contraception, the facts of abortion as well as childbirth. The needs of young people also include an environment where they can feel free to discuss the implications of sex as it relates to themselves.

The number of unwanted pregnancies is increasing, the number of abortions in young people is very high and yet the number of schools offering sex education to it's pupils is increasing also. What has gone wrong? I think that the major problem rests in our attitude toward sex education. Hitherto some teachers have believed that if you offer girls and boys facts about sex, this will arm them sufficiently to understand about conception and prevent it. This, of course, is pretty naive. In order to prevent conception several factors must be present. Obviously if girls are not having sex they cannot get pregnant, unless they are having some kind of petting so close to intercourse that they could be in danger without knowing it, so they have to know facts about insemination. If a girl has intercourse but is unaware of biological facts or, more likely, has a belief in old wives' tales of one sort or another, she also has to know the true facts. Most girls who get pregnant do not fall into these categories. They 'know' the facts and still get pregnant. Why?

There is not space in this book to go in depth into this subject, but the reasons for allowing a pregnancy may fall into some of these categories:

(1) The act of intercourse, in a very young and immature girl may seem like a game, a 'non-event' so that, as it hardly seems real then taking responsibility for it could not be at all necessary. 'It's mum as has the babies, not me'.

(2) The act may be seen as bad, and done against her better judgement, so that a pretence would have to be made that it was not happening, or alternatively a risk taken to enable punishment to be meted out.

(3) A girl might be so driven by the need to be 'needed' by the boy that all sense of self value would be lost in an effort to gain his pleasure and (temporary) regard. In this case she would not dare ask him to be responsible, would blind herself to her own danger.

(4) Unconsciously she might have a strong neurotic need to fulfil herself by a pregnancy. The neurotic reasons for needing a pregnancy are complex, some are almost consciously 'wanting a baby' or 'something to love', some are to do with the need

to prove womanhood, some are in response to some intensely complex family stress or parental anxiety.

(5) The relationship with the boy will offer difficulties in some cases. At one end of the scale the girl may almost consciously test him to see if he'll 'stand by her' or marry her if she gets pregnant. At the other, she may find the mutual roles of boy/girl very confusing and worry lest the boy will see her as too controlling if she uses birth control, or as too 'free' and likely to be promiscuous, so that she may hope that he will take responsibility and thus leave her in the passive 'feminine' position.

(6) The adolescent crisis often involves a good deal of rebellion against parental attitudes and sometimes because sexual activity is used in a rebellious spirit against parents then the delinquent content of the act may preclude taking responsibility for it.

Drugs

If I don't feel in a state of equilibrium, then I feel something is wrong and I try to re-establish equilibrium. There is a 'state of being' that is neither hyper-excited, over-happy, nor painful or sad. All people find it difficult to accept a change from this state and I think all people constantly seek to achieve it. In some cases it is fairly easy; if I am tired I rest until I am better; if I am hungry I eat. If I am cold I either put on more clothes, run around or light a fire. These are all realistic methods whereby physical ease can be obtained fairly easily, but if I have a burnt finger, a broken arm, or a headache, I may have to turn to somebody else to ease myself of pain. Some pains are fairly simply dealt with, some are not, so that the physician may have to use artificial aids to alleviate them. Thus I am given aspirin or alcohol or an anaesthetic. One of the aims of a highly civilized society seems to be in attempting to deny the necessity for pain or discomfort. People *expect* not to have pain, *expect* to be warm and well fed and well rested. So we expect of others, especially doctors, that they should achieve this for us, and the doctors thoroughly agree, being human themselves, and, with the assistance of phenomenal advertising campaigns, ladle out an astonishing number of pain killers.

But pain can be of several kinds and human response to pain can be valuable. When I was a child if I cut myself I not only suffered pain, I needed to be 'kissed better'. If the pain remained

I got very angry, and, like all children would blame something else for hurting me – that beastly knife, or more subtly, some*one* else, that beastly boy for laughing so that I fell off my bike, that beastly mother for not being sorry enough. As I got older I learned, perhaps, the futility of this projection, but perhaps I learned to blame myself instead. If I did not get enough love and attention I felt pain, the pain being unbearable would turn to fury, so that I would hate the parent who did not assuage my need, but if I hated that parent I might lose her for ever, so I learnt to keep my rage to myself. This fury unassuaged is the forerunner of depression.

In adolescence, when the boundaries of 'what is me' and 'what is other' are very insubstantial the unfocused pain, depression, self-hate, need for love, need for self-expression, need for understanding can be very frightening and very unpleasant. The adolescent has experienced the aspirin for the sore head, the 'medicine to make it better'. He has watched his parents take sleeping tablets, smoke cigarettes, drink alcohol to soothe them, has seen the doctor offer tranquilizers, has observed on hoardings, in films, on television, among teachers friends, in fact all around him, that, hopefully, if things are bad there is something you can take to make it better. People may not always comfort you, pain may not go of itself but 'taking something' will help.

Adults are very strange about drugs. They consume a very large part of the National Income by way of medicines, tobacco and drink, yet they are genuinely grieved and worried if their adolescents try to find a solution to their confusion by resorting to them. The word 'drug' to an adult means something bad which takes away from a person the drive to work, a sense of morality and purpose and sufficient taboos to keep sex contained. Adults have a picture of drug-takers as delinquent feckless drifters who will eventually die, yet the major cause of death in middle age can be attributed to drugs – to drink and tobacco and to an extent over-eating – i.e. to over-indulgence in substances that make a person 'feel better'.

There is, of course, some truth in the adult attitude for several reasons. Young people who take drugs *are* being rebellious. The 'drug culture' is, or until very recently was, a teen-age culture. Partly it is a teen-age response to what is seen as a bad and meaningless acquisitive society, partly to unloving and misunderstanding 'alienated' parents. Partly it is a deliberate act of rebellion against 'them', but no negative act would carry such a large proportion of a teen-age population with it unless it of itself was a help or at least was seen as a help to solve or ameliorate confused and unhappy feelings. Within the drug-taking culture, therefore, there are those young people who experiment 'because it is there', who take it 'because the others do' (the very necessary peer group acceptance), who hate the adult world and see drugs as a clever act of rebellion and those who seek from drugs a betterment of themselves and sometimes of others. Drugs, as I have said, are so much part of our society in one form or another that it would be surprising if young people did *not* use them.

Young people need to find a way to relate to themselves, to find themselves. The alienation from adults is a necessary part of this and so is the 'teen-age culture'. Within the various groups of teenagers the need for a solution to anxiety is represented in differing ways; among the rather bored, semi-illiterate, angry people, those who have little to look forward to and less to look back on, it would be tempting to find a way 'to have fun'. Excitement, a sense of being alive, of being on the scene, involved in real life and, at the same time, knowing that 'they' would disapprove, would be seen as enough in itself. If afterwards you felt really bad, tired out, depressed, empty, then never mind, the 'fun' can be had again. Amphetamines and the various analogous drugs could provide this. A whole night, two or three whole nights, spent awake, excited, unreserved, talkative, making friends – what more could a nervous, speechless, shy, lonely person want? Cheaper than alcohol, against the law and easily available. The pay-off comes when you find you can't sleep you are so high, so you take alcohol or 'sleepers' to blank out and get rest. The antihistamines, the barbiturates are generally used not by people who consciously try for a solution to problems but by those who can't face them. Barbiturates are at present extremely easy to obtain – they are, of course, available on prescription to anyone; the antihistamines are now far more difficult because responsible doctors have agreed not to prescribe them so that less are available. The effects of the various barbiturates vary, but in the long run they are, of course, soporific. A number of young people are now dependent upon them, and inject them intravenously for a quicker effect. The tablets are made up with chalk so that injection can be dangerous, causing severely thrombosed veins. There is a move at present for doctors to cease to prescribe barbiturates to patients, the argument being that they have now been superseded by other medicines. The major task of medical men and women, in my opinion, is to accept, and to help other people to accept that anxiety, unhappiness, sleeplessness and so on, are all part of life and that there is no need to pretend otherwise by annihilating feelings by artificial means, then the young might also move away from drugs themselves.

The young person on drugs is taking them because he does not know himself and the only relationship of which he is capable rests in the tenuous acceptance of a powerful peer group and ultimately with the needle and the substance injected by the needle.

Drugs of addiction such as heroin set yet another problem in that not only does life literally revolve around the relationship between the needle and the user, with all its concomitant semi-mystical paraphernalia, jargon and preparation, but also in the fact that the individual, at first feeling far, far better because of the drug coursing through his veins, then feels very bad indeed without it, and needs greater and greater doses to modify the misery. Physiological changes have taken place that make the body respond violently and unpleasantly to the drug's absence so that the person now feels far, far worse than before.

Whereas antihistamines give a sense of aliveness and excitement and barbiturates of calm and sleepiness mixed with excitement, marihuana and its derivatives have a slightly different effect. 'Pot' is smoked partly because it's a bit daring and illegal, partly because it's pleasant and partly, by some people, because it is claimed that while smoking, life can be seen more clearly, anger and hostility put to one side, peace, love and tranquillity achieved. It is more like the 'pipe of peace'. There is no doubt that the effect is pleasant, jokes funnier, people nicer, time elastic and no hang-over. There is no doubt that those people who smoke a good deal tend to do very little else, drop out from work, have diminished intellectual responses, less ability to use conceptualized thinking and are less sexually potent. It is very uncommon for violence to be present in a group of smokers. It is quite hard to define the problem of smoking. It may be that drop-outs do this before smoking, or that depressed people smoke *and* drop out, but like all artificial substances humans take in to increase enjoyment or diminish pain, smoking pot *does* cause deterioration. Smoking tobacco does also and so does alcohol. It is extremely difficult therefore to argue one way or the other as to whether 'pot' ought to be legal or illegal. Certainly a very large number of adults now smoke pot and do not appear to come to harm and a number do appear to. Reading statistics concerning heroin addiction one finds that practically all new addicts have previously taken other drugs, especially marihuana. Does that mean that the latter 'leads to' heroin? Certainly not. It could be argued that all heroin addicts have smoked tobacco, and that therefore tobacco 'leads' to heroin addiction, though there is obviously a higher correlation between pot-smoking and heroin than tobacco and heroin.

However, the 'sub-culture' that uses pot will inevitably include those who are unhappy enough to find pot disappointing and, within the culture of a 'drug-solution' and the sub-cultural peer group support, may be induced to move toward heroin. The teen-ager feels fragile, he feels impotent, lonely, unloved and angry, he *needs* to feel in a group and accepted by the group, he needs to feel better, he needs also to believe that heroin, or barbiturates, although potentially death-dealing to others, will not harm him because he can kick the habit when he wants to. He also needs to feel the adults don't want him and are hateful and repressive. So everything conspires, fantasies about the self and fantasies about other people, to induce in him a very real danger of experimenting.

Most teenagers experiment a little, very few get really deeply involved in drugs. Nearly always those who do have very severe distortions of personality, have *more* pain and sense of emptiness and *less* ability to form realistic relationships with other people, need in fact a false relationship 'with the needle' as the only one they can grasp and control themselves. Alcohol and cigarettes represent something rather different. Whereas drugs are seen by adolescents as part of their private world, their world into which adults cannot move, alcohol and cigarettes represent to them a way of stealing, as it were, adulthood from their elders. We have all, in our childhood played at being grown-up, in very early childhood we 'dressed up', then we played little mother and father games and later made up romantic plays to act or played doctors and nurses (usually as far as I can gather from discussing with others and matching my own memory the 'illness'

44

that needed treating was very near the genital region) but we knew it was 'only a game'. A number of us probably pinched a cigarette or two from our parents and smoked them (feeling pretty wicked and a bit sick) or even had an occasional swig at the bottle when no one was there, but these acts of delinquency were done really to test a little what it felt like, and also to be a bit daring.

However, when children even fool themselves into believing they *are* adults, so that the border-line between recognition of the game and the reality itself becomes blurred then one has to wonder why. There are numerous examples of the fact that although among middle-class young people adolescence seems to go on for a very long time, what with further education, university and so on, yet there is no doubt that childhood for a number of young people seems to offer so little after about the age of twelve, that there has to be a leap into a false adulthood as the only way to gain pleasure. The same problem is met with in sexual acting out. If at the same time the adolescent is angry with the adults around him, he can opt for adult ways as a method of cocking a snook – 'OK, smoking is for adults, drinking is for adults, well stop me if you can.'

Advertisements take up these intermixed themes very neatly. Most young people are lonely and feel awkward. They are shown the most delightful pictures of handsome, charming, rich, gay young people having a marvellous time drinking in pubs or often riding. Most young people are inhibited about sex and angry at the adults around them and they are shown pictures of wonderfully dressed girls enjoying the most extreme fantasies after drinking. In one advertisement they choose a particular drink that an older man would hate and it is stated that it's really a bit modern for an oldie.

So the external pressure is on: this is where the fun is, it's modern, it's good, and the oldies don't want us to enjoy it.

Alcoholism is increasing alarmingly in our society, and the amount of alcohol drunk by the young had gone up very fast. Even within ten years it has become commonplace for pubs to serve young people where before they never did. Does this matter? And what should be done?

I believe that any law which is not kept is a bad law. Either it is bad for young people to be given responsibility for their own decisions as regards smoking and drinking or it isn't bad. If it is bad, and the law by acknowledging it is bad, is formulated to protect young people, then it should be enforced. On the whole our laws are there to make us, as a population, feel more comfortable and to protect the weak. Some laws are out of date, but until changed they presumably represent a rough consensus of opinion in Great Britain. But it is odd how we are quite rigid about enforcing some laws (i.e. until recently against possessing marihuana) but extremely lax about the keeping of the law to do with serving under-age children alcoholic liquour. The difference lies of course at a realistic level, that whereas possession of marihunana is illegal for everybody, alcohol is only legal for special age groups, so that being not an absolute illegality it is very hard to enforce.

How does one therefore educate young people in order to prevent them from over-drinking? Every survey done on this subject correlates with surveys upon any other way in which young people attempt to solve their sense of unease: a child who has had good family and social experiences where alcohol is drunk in moderation in the home as a normal part of life (not as an escape *from* life) is far less likely to overdrink than the child who comes *either* from a home so rigid that drink is seen as horrible, evil, etc., etc., *or* from one where really nobody cares, and, especially, where a member of the family is a really heavy drinker and causes thereby a problem – either financial, emotional, mental, aggressive or all combined.

Whatever the behaviour problem examined the preventive measures seem comparable. The child who feels bad will very frequently see the solution as outside himself and if he doesn't find it, i.e. in a 'better' school or club, in delinquency and exciting driving of stolen cars, in aggression, in pacificism and vegetarianism, in sex, he may, in despair, seek it in tranquillizers and exciters, in drugs and alcohol. So that, in the school situation it would seem to me that neither denial nor over-emphasis of any problem is sensible, but patient and quiet dialogue about the matter and the offering to the child of respect and esteem and acknowledgement of the pressures put upon him without and from within.

CHAPTER 5

Pregnancy

I have already described some of the complex reasons why a girl may get pregnant. It may be that it would be useful to examine the types of solution to this crisis for a girl still in school. Now that abortion is legally one solution, the decision-making process around what to do about the pregnancy becomes a very important issue. What I propose to examine is

(1) what the pregnancy and potential child means to the schoolgirl herself;

(2) what it means to the family;

(3) how the school might be affected;

(4) how our society is affected;

(5) what the potential child may experience if born.

The pregnant schoolgirl

In order to help a girl who is pregnant to come to a decision with which she can live I would want to know several things. I would attempt to find out with the girl what the pregnancy meant to her. In doing this I think I would gain a good deal of insight into her maturity, strengths and sense of reality. Let me quote a story to illustrate this.

A girl of 16 came to see me seeking a termination of pregnancy. I already knew something about her. She was West Indian, she had had difficulties at home, then had been received into care. I also knew her as she had in the past received birth control advice from me.

I asked her what she felt like when she first realized she was pregnant, and she replied she was thrilled to bits, to think she'd been able to do it, she was actually *pregnant*. And she added that she'd always wanted a baby, something of her own and something to love as she never felt she'd had much love herself. She hadn't thought much about school because she was leaving soon and couldn't care less, and she hadn't thought much about her parents as they couldn't care less. As the days went by, however, she began to look at the life-style of one of her friends who had a baby. She had always envied this girl the child, but, perhaps because she was now identifying with moterhood more, she saw very gradually the very real difficulties. She described how one night she and her friend were due to go out with their boyfriends and the difficulties they experienced in getting the child to settle and 'there we were, boy friends jeering and saying they weren't waiting there all day, baby screaming whatever we did, gave it a bottle, changed its nappy – when it puked down my mate's blouse I suddenly realized which way the love had got to go. I wasn't going to get love *from* my baby. I had got to give love *to* her and to tell you the truth I haven't any to give, *I'm* the one that wants loving, so once my kid stopped sleeping all day and started wanting something from me, I'd want to wring its neck, so you see doctor, I can't have this baby, it wouldn't do any good'. I think this is a most revealing statement. It expresses so clearly the factors involved in why she wanted a pregnancy (to be like her friend, to prove womanhood, to spite her family, to get away from school and to be *loved*) and how she was able to see that the baby would have needs of its own that she could not fulfil.

Another girl of 15 was sent to see me by the school counsellor. She was pregnant, her mother wanted her to have a termination, the school thought it advisable, but she wanted the baby. I got to know this girl quite well. She was having great difficulties at home with a very punitive father whom she knew was unfaithful to his wife and with whom I think she had a very strong and difficult relationship. She had run away from home and called in the police and social services to protect her at times. She was adamant that she would not return, that her boy-friend, although delinquent and 'in trouble' would live with her, find a flat, share with the baby, and look after her, that she could get a job (and that the school would turn a blind eye to her age). Over the next few weeks Mary gradually became aware of her need for her mother (who still wanted her to have an abortion). She still, in effect, *felt* very young. She also became aware that flats are difficult to get, her boy-friend was not all that stable and, above all, that she would find it appallingly difficult at her age to cope with all this without her mother and with a baby. She had a termination, did, for a while, find a flat and live with her boy-friend, but gradually realizing how hard it all was, drifted back home again.

Not finding home quite as before, she again felt restless and unhappy and again tried to live with her boy-friend. She stopped taking the 'pill' and came again to see me believing herself to be pregnant. She told me that she was delighted, that her boy would stand by her and that all would now be wonderful. In fact I did not confirm her pregnancy, but curiously enough the second time she came she told me the boy was angry when she told him she'd been to see me, and started shouting at her and hitting her in case she was pregnant. She was now faced with two imponderables. She wanted to be pregnant and she wanted the boy to accept her and her baby, but in fact she wasn't pregnant. In a curious confusion she left me very angrily as though her *lack* of pregnancy was my fault, and left the boy because if she *had* been pregnant he would have been furious.

Both these girls were able at times to view the pregnancy in fairly realistic terms. They could grasp what it might be like to have a child and what changes it would make in their own lives. Having reached this level of conceptualizing, they could make a decision based upon it that could have relevance and, after the termination they would then hopefully be able to acknowledge the decision as one that at the *time* was appropriate. They might, and indeed would, at times wish they had decided differently, they might sometimes be regretful and sad, but at least the experiences would have been *real*. In the case of the second girl, alas, she could not contain the experience and learn from it. Her second attampt at a pregnancy was itself based upon totally unreal fantasies as to the boy's likely response, and her anger at me for not confirming her in her desires evoked a typically childlike response.

Elizabeth on the other hand, shows how a different approach can produce a quite sad situation. Elizabeth was an adopted child. She became pregnant when she was 16. Her adoptive parents, who had only told her the facts of her early history fairly recently, were very kind to her. They explained that of course she had better stay in a home for mothers and babies for a little while so that no one need know what had happened, that she would then have the baby and have it adopted without ever being made to see it, thus making other parents as happy as they had been made when Elizabeth was given to them. All went according to plan, the baby was born with ease and was taken away immediately. The girl went home and was lovingly received by her parents.

However, she found herself terribly upset and tearful. She missed the baby overwhelmingly and was constantly worrying what it looked like, whether it was well cared for and what it would have been like to keep it. Her parents could not understand any of her behaviour. They pointed out how lucky she was, having such kindly parents, how fortunate she had been in not being forced to see the baby and how amazingly happy she had made a childless couple. So they insisted she dry her tears and act more appropriately. Two years later she became pregnant again. This time, remembering all that had gone before, she determined to make all the decisions herself. She was aware how angry she had been that at no time did her parents consult her wishes. She went to her GP and demanded a termination. He rather tiredly wrote a note immediately to the hospital, conveying to the girl that he was pretty fed up with girls who came to see him, wasting his time with these demands. She went to the hospital and had a very brief interview with a doctor. In effect he accepted her demand and hoped that at least *this* time she'd learn at last not to be so irresponsible.

When she came out of hospital and returned to the flat she shared with friends, they were most alarmed at her behaviour. She became extremely depressed and hysterical at times. She cried and raved and attempted to slash her wrists; she tore the curtains and threw cushions around, or lay inert on a bed all day. One of them brought her to the Centre. Towards the end of a long interview, she discussed all the difficulties she had had in the past by not being allowed to experience her own feelings. In her first pregnancy nobody had asked *how* she was or tried to understand how she felt. She had never been able to tell anyone how guilty she was at paining her parents; how at the time she thought it was 'bad blood' coming out from her inheritance, the fact that she, also, was illegitimate. She had worried and worried about who her 'real' mother was and had never been able to ask. When she became pregnant she had wondered whether a termination would be a solution but no-one had let her consider it. She never saw the baby nor, therefore, knew what it looked like nor what it felt like to be a mother. She was unable to grieve over the loss of the baby partly because it had scarcely seemed real, partly because she was supposed to be happy that she had given other people pleasure.

All this maternal feeling came pouring out, and, with it, a sense of surprise that although at her second pregnancy she *had* made the decision, yet she still felt so terrible. I pointed out to her that unfortunately it seemed to me she had *not* in fact been given an opportunity to think through her decision. Both the doctors she had seen had accepted her assumption *a priori* and neither had given her time to look at the reality of her predicament nor to see its relation to her first pregnancy. At no time in either pregnancy had she therefore been able to feel her way into a decision. The first time her parents had disallowed it, the second, she herself.

Fairly soon after this, with one or more consultations, she became quite well again and was able to return to normal behaviour and a sense of well-being.

It is difficult for adults to know how to respond when a girl says she is pregnant. An adult may be assaulted by a whole series of conflicting feelings. The situation as described by the young person may arouse feelings of anger or of comparison – 'How could she be such a fool as to let it happen?' 'How could *he* be such a monster not to look after her?' 'Serves her right if she goes to all-night parties and gets drunk.' 'It's all the parents' fault for not loving her enough – being strict enough – telling her enough.' 'Of course she always was a selfish – wild – unprincipled girl.' 'It's so awful for the parents.' 'It's so awful for the other children.' All these thoughts are, alas, though understandable, not only irrelevant but subjective. Underneath these attitudes there may lie very real but almost unconscious feelings of anger against the girl. 'What has she done that *I* never did, enjoyed herself? How dare a mere *child* experience what I didn't? How dare she be grown up, it is *my* generation that is'. There is very real pain for men and women in the acknowledgement of their own feelings of envy and anger. The response to the young person, therefore, may well be a response to the adult's feelings *about* the situation and not a true response *to* the situation. If this human response is not examined then the individual may not be free to offer real help.

A parent faced with a pregnant daughter is bound to be emotional, upset and angry. Her response varies according to her temperament. It can range from over-competence – Well, we'll just have to get it terminated – through Oh, you poor darling – Oh, you *fool* – Look what it's done to your father/mother /sister/grandmother – to What will the neighbours say – Of course it may mean you'll never be able to get a decent man again – have another baby – live with us any more – get a university entrance, etc., etc. The average parent, having blown off steam in one manner or another can almost always find a way, because of the affection that is present, to be supportive and caring, but may find it very difficult *not* to make the decision as to outcome for the child.

The doctor it would seem to me, is in a much clearer position, or should be. He represents a respected profession which carries within it a body of fairly precise knowledge. He can therefore give a factual account of the state of the pregnancy and the development of the baby or the facts of abortion. He can also because he is trusted, give an opinion as to his own attitude concerning the possible solutions but what he must be very honest about to the young person is the difference between medical and moral opinions. A skilled doctor has to be able to do so, I think, because he is now called upon to act as a true counsellor, to enable the client more fully to look into her *own* feelings and to test *with* her whether she is capable of making decisions for herself that she can stand by. It is very easy to wrap up a personal opinion in medical jargon and present it as fact. I believe that a number of doctors are able to counsel, a number are not. The doctor is under great pressure from the client and her parents to collude with the decision, to make it *for* them and ease the burden in this way, but he is not in a position to do this. The client's decision will become part of her history so that she alone can be responsible for it.

It can be immensely difficult, however, if the person before you is very deprived, very disordered or very young, for the ability to make realistic and permanently valid decisions may be very small.

Let us examine some of these problems. If, as I have suggested, the early adolescent has very great difficulty in distinguishing behaviour reality and fantasy; if she is still so bound to the family group feelings that she finds it difficult not to respond and act in relation to these feelings, then a pregnancy is almost inevitable if intercourse takes place, as I have suggested, because either intercourse is a game or a defence against feelings of inadequacy or an act of defiance against parents or in response to real or imagined peer group pressure. In none of these situations would the act be recognized as a responsible one. If, when the pregnancy occurs the young person is still in this situation, and why not?, she will respond to it in a comparable manner. She may deny it has happened until she can do so no longer because it's self-evident – either because it doesn't *seem* to have happened 'really' or because the recognition of it would, in her eyes, destroy her parents or herself. She may be pleased it has happened and weave fantasies about the happiness that will ensue, with a nice flat, a nice boy and a lovely baby, or no boy, but nice parents, or no parents but a lovely baby.

She may be so frightened that it has happened that she runs away from home or she may consult her friends and act upon their opinion by either going ahead and having it, or seeking termination. A very young girl precipitated into a situation too profound to deal with will therefore very likely choose or drift into a 'pseudo decision'. School-children may well, therefore, wish to have their babies but find after they are born that they can neither deal with an adoption nor with the responsibilities of motherhood. If the young immature girl is also responding to unrequited needs for love and sees the baby as fulfilling these needs, she may well decide to have her baby and, as described earlier, recognize too late that she cannot tolerate the child's demands upon her. If she has a termination, on the other hand, the whole process may be so meaningless that nothing has been gained of adulthood through the experience. Those young people who get pregnant while in a state of childlike unreality may not be able to assimilate the reality of a pregnancy nor a birth. Second pregnancies so very often result if the reason for the first has not been established. I don't mean the obvious reason – that no birth control was used, that the girl was drunk, or raped, but the very much more important fundamental reason, that the girl needed a pregnancy.

If we are confronted, therefore, with a girl whom we suspect cannot make a real decision, do we accept whatever she believes she wants, or make up her mind for her?

Jasmine was a very difficult girl, she was suspended from school, she went out with a man much older than herself who came from a poverty-stricken 'mucky' family. She quarrelled bitterly with her step-father, her mother found her very upsetting. If only, the mother would say, Jasmine could see how silly she is, wanting to leave school at 16 and marry that awful man.

She'll always be poor and she'll not ever enjoy life. Look what she could do if she stayed on, have a decent career, nice clothes and a *good* life. The mother would add that when she looked back on her own life she bitterly regretted not having had a career to turn to when her first husband died. Jasmine didn't want a career. She hated school and hated home. She just wanted to be married and have heaps of kids. Eventually she became pregnant. She wanted her baby – she saw herself marrying the minute she could and declared passionately that abortion was murder. She became more and more sad as her mother increased the pressure upon her to have an abortion. Jasmine said it would be murder, her mother said that she herself would die if Jasmine went ahead. She affirmed that she would commit suicide or her husband leave her. In the end Jasmine gave way because a doctor at a hospital pointed out to her how young and selfish she was in making her mother so unhappy, insisted upon admitting her within a few days and performed the operation. Jasmine was extremely depressed and angry afterwards and had very unhappy nightmares. Within a year she had had a baby and married.

This is not the end of Jasmine's story. I have, however, by using this illustration, tried to establish the complexity of people's responses to a critical situation. The mother *did* project her own frustration upon her daughter, she *did* blackmail her, she *did* force a decision upon her. Nevertheless it may well be that if Jasmine had had her baby and fought against its adoption, she would have found marriage and a child more difficult that she had supposed. It may be that if she had allowed the baby to be adopted she would have been just as depressed and angry and taken the same course. So that I think we must accept that there is scarcely ever a 'right' decision, or a 'wrong' one. Just that if we can marginally help a young person to increase their maturity, examine their natures and their needs at the time of crisis we may have done as much as is possible.

There is considerable evidence that second pregnancies do occur more often in young, rather dull, lower-class children. Perhaps we could work harder to educate these young people concerning not so much the facts of intercourse but the outcome for them. Perhaps we could give them a sense of self-esteem as well as self-awareness so that they didn't need to have intercourse until it could be a really joyful experience – perhaps we could help to give them some other life style other than sexual availability or maternity which would be more fulfilling, I don't mean unreal goals of becoming doctors or nurses, but the really valid sense of self-importance, self-esteem and self-respect.

Teachers are in a rather different position. Their personal response to the recognition of a pregnancy may well be the same, in that after all every man and woman, whatever their position in life, responds initially in a manner peculiar to themselves but there has to be a secondary response in relation to the facts of their situation. Sometimes people are blinded by the external situation or their appraisal of it and cannot allow their own feelings to be honestly examined. It is easier to say what I must hold on to is what's right for the school than to separate out the strands of a complex set of reactions, some based upon personal anguish or acceptance, some upon the very real need to look at the girl and the institution in which both are placed.

A teacher, therefore, faced with a girl who is pregnant may well be able appropriately to advise and counsel. It may well be that the trust the girl places in her is justified. Sadly, girls, partly because of guilt, partly a need to see 'the other' as bad or unfeeling frequently make it very hard for the teacher – either refusing to talk, behaving abominably or pretending they don't mind.

The decision as to the outcome has to be made in collaboration with parents and doctor, of course, but the method of dealing with the knowledge of the pregnancy is a necessary part of teaching. If the fact can be kept confidential then obviously it should be. If the girl tells her friends, that's her affair. If rumours spread it becomes a teacher's affair. If the teacher can genuinely see the problem as a crisis for the girl she can always handle the class appropriately. If the teacher sees the pregnancy as disgusting and shameful then her feelings will emerge and be a part of an unhealthy confusion of issues.

If a girl decides to continue with her pregnancy and have her baby – what should the school's reaction be?

There is no direct answer to this. Looking first at the *girl's* needs, I think that with careful and forthright discussion within the school, discussion involving the girl and her parents, the girl can gradually be helped to form an opinion as to what would seem best.

A process as miraculous as pregnancy can never of itself be shameful. I am quite certain that no 'bad influence' could ever spread in a school if a girl continued as a pupil. The effect upon the other pupils will, of course, be complex. Some will be shocked, some compassionate, some envious, but a healthy school should, I think, be able by its own surety of approach to enable the other pupils to mature more ably, not less. The ability of a headmistress and of the staff to accept the girl as a pupil, accept their own primary task as that of education, will go a long way to relieve anxiety. If as well as this the girl is neither feted nor ignored, but seen as a normal pupil, albeit in particular and fundamentally joyful, though at the same time problematic circumstances, the best will be engendered in the children.

The pregnant girl herself deserves to enjoy her pregnancy. Certainly she very likely feels worried, rather ashamed, doubtful and often frustrated and angry that this new state has come upon her. But the act of creation should still be a very amazing one. It may be that a considerable change will take place in the girl's attitude to her external surroundings and towards herself. She will have a good deal of complex feelings about her family and her friends. She may well have an added burden of a rejecting boy-friend, or a boy-friend whom her family reject. She may become very introspective, drawn in, perhaps to her own surprise to share, as it were, the growing baby with herself. Studying may be quite difficult or seem irrelevant. Intellectual thought, especially if seen as a method for career achievement, may seem silly and a waste of time. The assumption of 'womanhood' may make school seem absurd. I think there is no rule at all as to how a pregnant girl 'should' behave. The younger the girl the less likely she will be to be able to experience pregnancy in all its depths. It may be that a residential school or home tuition would be better for her than to stay at school.

The main reason for any decision as to placement would seem to me to rest upon what, basically, would be best for the girl, but obviously recognition must be given to external factors.

Parents cannot always manage to accept a pregnancy. They have very real and understandable pain and anger. It may well be that a refuge elsewhere would be in the child's interest until the family can sort out their feelings.

I remember a girl coming to me demanding a termination 'because it would kill her mother if she knew so she couldn't *have* the baby'. Another girl said she mustn't have a termination because if her mother found out she would kill her. Upon being asked how the mother would respond to the pregnancy, she said that, too, must be kept secret, but that when the baby was born it would be all right because her mother, naturally, loved all babies and once she saw it she'd come round.

The boy-friend is scarcely ever involved in decision-making. I think this a very great pity. Beneath the fear-response of denial or running away there lie far deeper and more important sentiments. A boy who causes a pregnancy often feels absolutely delighted at first. He was proved his masculinity. This attitude is quite common and overt in West Indian boys, who would beat up a girl rather than allow her to have an abortion, even though they might not be willing to take any emotional or financial responsibilty either for the mother or the child.

A second response will of course be that of rejection – refusal to accept the pregnancy as theirs, anger at the girl for letting it happen, or frank 'well, it's her affair, let her get on with it', but I believe that it is *never* valuable to accept superficial responses as the whole story. If a boy is brought into the situation by a family, or, if the family can't bear it, by a counsellor, then, he, too may gain in maturity by recognizing that the crisis involves him as much as her.

It is less common for girls to wed a boy because she is pregnant than heretofore and indeed unless the couple were genuinely ready for marriage apart from the acknowledgement of the crisis of pregnancy then marriage would seem scarcely ever the solution. A boy and girl, not yet in charge of their own personalities, not yet sure of their own characters, needs and anxieties, could only bring to marriage a fantasy of commitment and a difficulty in seeing the partner as real. I have no doubt that some young people will continue to marry whether pregnant or not and that there will be occasions when married school-children are more than a rarity, but the statistics for the breakdown of marriage are highly significantly correlated with youthfulness.

When the baby is born a new set of difficulties arise. I will not embark upon a detailed discussion of the problems of school-girl mothers. The Working Party chaired by Dame Margaret Miles will no doubt draw attention to them and make recommendations; as far as schooling is concerned it would seem to me that a child has a right to choose and that this choice should not be hampered by external difficulties. A mother has a right to look after her baby if she can and she has a right to education if she wishes. One of the great difficulties encountered in dealing with adolescents, as I have mentioned several times, rests in their difficulties in understanding the difference between real and fantasy and in their very great difficulty in seeing a solution as a long-term thing. Every difficulty must be solved at the moment it is encountered, the containment of frustration, the planning and learning slowly is almost unendurable. A young mother will reflect this in all manner of ways. She will expect her baby to behave beautifully and be 'hers' to be proud of, at the same time she will want her mother to take it if it's a bore or difficult. She will want to go out with the boys and have fun and at the same time be left alone to be a mother and not be lectured to. She will believe that by giving up school she'll never have a career or that school is a stupid waste of time. She will in fact be unable to accept that she has time, that her circumstances will change. This leads her into various mistaken actions. She may try to live alone with the baby, she may try living at home, she may 'put baby in a nursery', she may give up boys – she may hate the baby for preventing her from enjoying girlhood. The changing attitudes and feelings are absolutely characteristic of adolescents and would be quite understandable if the enforced maternity did not necessitate a fair constancy of environment and feeling on behalf of the baby. Bringing up a child demands maturity, bringing one up without a husband demands enormous self-awareness and strength. Bringing it up within the family demands a very high level of understanding of the mutual and often contradictory roles of grandparents, mother and child, and adolescents almost certainly will not have all these qualities.

Financially they will also be at a severe disadvantage – even if they can claim Social Security benefit (and at present they cannot always) it will be small. If they go to work the money will be pitiful. Rents are high, housing in large urban areas costly.

It may seem unnecessary to discuss the problems of young motherhood in a book primarily for teachers, but I think it essential in order that the girl can be seen in a larger setting than that of the school.

The greater society, the town or village or state, will also determine to a very great extent the manner in which a pregnancy be handled. Each nation, each class, each individual has its own mores. What is shameful in one generation seems normal in another. A Cypriot family will respond entirely differently from a

Jamaican, a Nigerian, an English or a Jewish. No family is entirely free of the pressure of it's own society, however heterodox, so that a decision made today by a family will be one determined partly by the attitude of the larger group and partly the attitude of the larger group will be determined by the new responses of its families. Change therefore will be continual and multi-factional, so that although we might seek to clear our own minds of individual prejudices and attitudes and to help the girl or boy to clear theirs, yet the distinction between what is 'really' me and what is society can be very blurred and difficult to define.

A society can never be perfect, and a school can never be, nor can an individual. If we see pregnancy as a sign of a sick society, a bad school, a bad parent or a bad child we are lost at one level. We try and find out *why* it happens and because society deems it unfortunate we try to prevent it, but it seems to me that if we seek too deeply for causes and either place the blame on ourselves or society or the child, then we cannot move forward.

Perhaps the best we can do is to accept that people and parti-cularly adolescents, are pretty frail, make awful mistakes but as a whole want the good, then we can allow for muddle and noise and confusion both within and without. It is far easier to establish a primary goal than to be confused by contradictory and complex ones. I am often asked 'and what about the poor baby?' and I do very sincerely believe that we must not lose sight of the rights of the child.

A baby needs a secure, loving home. We have encountered over and over again adults who cannot be at peace or allow society to be at peace, because they are so empty, so angry and so scarred.

So ought we to decide *for* a young person what is right, basing our assumption upon our view of the baby's needs? I don't know. I *do* know that the only way I can work is to try and establish with a young person as best I can what it may be like for her in relation to the various choices open to her and to explore with her what a pregnancy means to her that she allowed it to happen. A child can mature very rapidly when faced with such reality as a pregnancy. We have no right to take this maturational chance from the child. Our task is to judge as best we may, at what point the child is incapable of further choice and at that point to assist her, not before.

CHAPTER 6

The role of adults in society.
The law and delinquency

There is no doubt in my mind that human beings need terms of reference. The more immature the individual, the greater the need.

In a static society these terms of reference were relatively permanent. In reading *Larkrise to Candleford*[5] one is struck by the unalterability of village life and yet made aware that in fact already great changes were taking place. The economy had changed and very gradually the inhabitants of the village themselves changed in their expectations. Nevertheless there was a kind of consensus of what was 'done' and what was not. Within this society people were, of course, very different. Some were marvellous housewives, some hopeless. Some men were good workmen and good husbands, some were deplorable, but there was a homogeniety which allowed for differences while offering a fairly flexible matrix. In reading of the *Family & Kinship Patterns in East London*[6] one is again very struck by the surprisingly well-established family tie system still existing. You can find it in the description of the life of the Kray Brothers and countless novels of middle class life portray this. The rigidity of some aspects of middle class life lays a stranglehold upon its people, but there is a very real vigour and liveliness in the genuine working-class patterns. It is a bit of a myth to assume that all this has broken down. There are innumerable families who still visit one another regularly, live nearby, follow the same trades and professions, advise, counsel, support and condemn one another. Families that I have known, for instance, living in an area notorious for its drifting and delinquent population who have established themselves for several generations, whose cousins, aunts, grandparents still know each other and share problems with one another. Many of the characters described by Dickens were, on the contrary, totally alone or alienated from their family group, so that I think we should be careful when we make assumptions that the family and the extended family has broken down recently.

A hundred years ago I believe *more* women worked than do now. Mary Ward House was set up partly to give an opportunity for children to play in safety while their mothers worked rather than roam the streets.

There *is* of course more geographical mobility, but not all families move to new towns, get jobs in other places or emigrate. It was quite commonplace in a North London borough to find families who had never crossed a main road half a mile away and certainly many South London people had not crossed the river.

However, it does seem that in general there is a loosening up of ties. Old people are looked after by their families less than before (though this could be partly explained by the fact that they live longer and reading nineteenth century literature one is struck forcibly how often the old landed up 'on the Parish' in the workhouse). Children do have different values from those of their parents and marriages break up far more than they ever did. Families are also smaller (though one must not forget the very high infant and adult mortality rate in the past which decimated many families).

The feudal paternalistic system, rigid and unfair as it was, did offer the poor and the defenceless some degree of protection and security. The rapidly increasing town population presented an entirely different picture. Nobody cared for anybody because there were not such direct responsibilities. The intelligent, kindly women who gradually took over the function of the head of the village in towns, who distributed food, clothing and education and offered lodgings to the 'deserving poor' who, in spite of very patronizing exhortations, nevertheless were a very real help, are highly characteristic of life in the second half of the nineteenth century.

The social services developed of course from these early beginnings and very soon, certainly in the case of Mary Ward for example, the women were recognizing that patronizing the poor was humiliating and debilitating and that the function of the social worker must be to help them to find their own solutions, not to offer largesse. From this developed the various 'grass roots' methods and the case-work techniques. It is always appropriate that people recognize abuses of human freedom and dignity and combine together to ensure social change. There must always be a body of people who are watchful of inequalities, of inappropriate and unfair behaviour and of the need for special services.

The housing problems have highlighted this fact for example. It is not true that 'anyone' can obtain housing if they try. 'Anyone' can't. There are special groups with particular needs for whom housing must be obtained and groups quite rightly form to point out the absurdity of empty houses and concomitant homelessness. People, however, grow by extending themselves. Meeting a challenge is a self-developing process and kindly people would do a disservice to those in need if they *only* made provision for them.

However, some people, because of age, immaturity, deprivation, neurosis or inadequacy cannot achieve a satisfying life without help. In some cases the provision of a service – such as a house to live in – is enough; in others more is needed – some understanding of the deeper needs of the person, some recognition that potentialities can be developed with help, but that in certain cases, the support needed for individuals may have to be pretty long term. Nevertheless, I believe whatever support we offer, support used as a term to differentiate from treatment, we must all offer just enough that the individual can take as much responsibility for himself as is possible. 'Man's reach must exceed his grasp.'

In any move from autocracy toward democracy there is bound to be a time when order appears to be giving way to chaos, there are bound to be people who cannot manage and those who are over-disruptive and over-destructive. We, as individuals and as members of a democracy, try to find a way to live at peace with people who are not always peaceful, to share with people who seem greedy, to collaborate with those who are self-willed, so that it is harder in some ways for the individual who feels he does know where he is going. Perhaps our greatest strength lies in our ability to accept individualization, but not anarchy. We learn to live with each other, not wishing to force people to be what they are not nor so careless of their welfare that we lack the desire to help, but we also recognise the validity of our personal desire to achieve and have a good life.

It would be very dishonest if, in the guise of freedom, we stood back and did nothing. It is painfully easy to use words to hide a lack of concern and to put responsibility as far away from ourselves as possible. A parent who lets a child 'do as he likes' is not in fact loving that child. A society which removes all restraints from the matrix, does as much disservice to the young and the weak as the society which is so rigidly constructed

62

that no individual can feel free. Caring means the offering of support and love when necessary and the encouragement of the individual to take responsibility for himself. A democracy has to be flexible. At some point restraints must be evident and available, not for the sake of restraining but of containing. So that a responsible society is one in which people can live in freedom and recognize that self-restraint is the goal for all, but other restraint must be offered at times. Permissive does not mean anarchic. It suggests rather that a society allows people to be what they are, to offer each other what they can, to be respected as individuals. If one respects a person, one also must set limits for that person if he can't do so for himself. Then one can achieve true co-operation, so that by allowing people to be themselves, we achieve a corporate sense, co-operative and not over-ambitious.

Adolescents are loud, noisy, exuberant, over-active, self-centred and dismissive of idiots. They are also unsure, idealistic, desperately aware of their failures and sensitive to criticism. A society that pretends to offer freedom to the young but in fact offers a vacuum, will get the young it deserves. The young *can* be co-operative, their aggression and noise and exuberance can be allowed freedom of expression in so many ways that enhance their sense of value, their sense of prowess, their sense of imaginative creativity. Instead of being afraid of adolescence and turning our backs on them, instead of trying to hold them back in infancy, why don't we co-operate with them to remove some of society's worst problems?

The law and delinquency

The legal system of a country reflects fairly accurately its moral and economic position. Most of the inhabitants of the globe now adhere to the principle of possession and promulgate laws to ensure the safety of these possessions. Our society also believes in the rights of man to live at peace, have choice in his work, his beliefs, and his general mode of life to an extent. Laws reflect this. It is legally 'wrong' to steal, we have free elections and we protect our citizens against being physically molested or killed. Laws may reflect moral attitudes but they do not of themselves provide moral absolutes. If I kill my brother I am put in prison. If I kill my country's enemy I am given a medal. There are laws designed to protect the individual against himself; it used to be illegal to commit suicide and if not successful the culprit would be brought before the court. It is illegal to smoke marihuana, illegal for a child not to go to school, for a girl under a certain age to have sex or have an abortion unless certain legal restrictions have been fulfilled. It is illegal to be married to two women and used to be illegal for a man to have sex with another man. It is illegal for a woman to sell herself on the street.

Laws therefore are designed to protect our property and to protect ourselves against others and against ourselves.

It is quite difficult at times to dissociate the moral quality from the legal. If a child does not go to school it is against the law, is he therefore doing wrong? If he steals my car is he doing wrong in the moral sense? I suppose he is if there is general consensus that our needs and aims as a society represents the general good and therefore anyone putting any part of our society at risk is in that respect 'wrong'.

The manner in which we develop moral community values is complex. I suppose that we do so roughly because we want to be accepted. In very early infancy our mothers can withold love and endearments in relation to our behaviour and we soon know this.

By the time a child reaches school age he has a pretty good notion of the values of society. He must 'share' his toys. He must do as he is told, not be jealous, not kick and scream, not be greedy, not be selfish, in fact he must learn the validity of other people's needs and feelings. If the lessons have been learnt in a household which obviously offers a fair consistency and love, he will thrive and in spite of the curbs upon his spontaneity, be able to expand, explore and enjoy his life. If his household has offered contrariness, anger, uncaringness or a very tight restraint, then he will not have been able to learn inner control at all or only at the cost of a withering of his personality.

All children want to explore; the task of the adult is to enable them to do so while maintaining a stable environment and without damaging themselves.

When we were children we all had temper tantrums, we lied, we fought, we stole, we smashed. We were rude, dirty and demanding. Gradually because we met with the adult veto, we desisted and were able to accept our relationship to the whole without too much loss. We learnt in fact that we were *not* the whole, we were not even the other half of the mother, filling her complete world, but we were a part of a family and a society and abided by its laws in order that *we* could feel better. We developed a conscience which later would contain our greed and fury even when external restraints were not put upon us unless the external situation became unbearable, or the internal world too chaotic and oppressive.

It might therefore be argued that there are several kinds of delinquency:

(1) The explorative – A boy climbs a fence into a yard, partly because it's fun anyway and he's got little else to do, partly because it's a challenge physically, partly because his mates 'dare' him to and partly to risk being found out. It also might be good sport to get whatever is there and bring it out. If he is caught and some sanction placed upon him, he may decide it's not worthwhile doing it and will have 'learned his lesson'. He might, alternatively find this type of 'dare' a bit silly and 'childish' or might find alternative pleasures such as football, rock climbing, karate, etc. He might be said to have 'grown out of it'. It would be very unlikely that he would have a conscience about depriving the owner of the yard of his goods, though in other situations this might be so. So that he stops his delinquency because of several factors:

Society has set limits – or he is 'stopped'.

Maturity has set alternative goals that are more valuable to *him*.

His conscience has shown him that his act has caused another pain.

(2) The 'psychopathic' to use the word very loosely. The boy described before gets caught and 'punished'. He repeats his crime. He takes articles from a shop and sells them for some ludicrous sum. He is in a group with other youths and takes purses from housewives' shopping bags at bus-stops. He gets fined, he gets 'sent away'. He comes back from 'being away', he attends a local school and behaves so badly he is suspended. He goes to another school but truants, to the pleasure to be honest of the staff who are totally fed up with him. What of this lad? Society, or individuals have 'caught' him and he is still delinquent. He has been offered alternative methods of dealing with his exuberance and need to explore and dare: he has been shown

the pain to which he has put the housewives. He has been 'given every opportunity' but somehow he has never 'learnt'. It is as though something is lacking; the conscience – the self-contained discipline, the ability to deflect into more valuable maturational activities. This type of delinquent may still 'grow out of it' or may, with luck, find someone who can enable him to accept inner and outer controls; sometimes this person is a relation, sometimes a work-mate or a teacher, sometimes a social worker, often a girl-friend.

There is no doubt that a complex and flexible society which is liberal in intention must put up with a considerable amount of delinquent activity. Nevertheless it would be absurd to reach a stage of apathy where the whole population vaguely let it happen and did nothing about it, hoping it would pass. Draconic remedies such as have been used in the past, hanging, beating and long-term imprisonment, not only are now seen as cruel and archaic but also as unsuccessful. Modern methods seem to be based upon an assumption that people are delinquent for *reasons*, reasons not to do with evil or self-will, but to do with unconscious factors within the individual and with an expression of a sick society or environment.

An acquisitive society will teach that possessions are important and that you gain status by gaining them. A society which apparently does not care for people will produce people who do not care for society. A child who is unloved will hate. A child who has known no limits will not be able to be self-limiting but also a child who has been over-restricted will burst out. The checks and balances of a relatively healthy society will offer the average child sufficient concern and respect, sufficient freedom and sufficient restraints that he can establish a fulfilled life; but no society can do this completely. There will be angry, bored and restless young people and we as adults must find a way to make life tolerable for ourselves, while attempting to offer the child a better perception of himself and the world.

Persistent delinquents therefore are a puzzle. Why do they continue to go against the law in spite of the punishments we mete out and the help we offer? The answer must lie in the interaction between the self and the other. If I am starving, however moral I may be, I may well, to save my life, steal food. If I am starving of love, I may try to steal that and I will deal with neurotic delinquency in the next part, but if I am only half aware of my potential, feel vaguely unsure, vaguely angry at 'them', have never learnt the value of considering another because no one has genuinely considered *me*, then I will continue to do as I like and take what I like because it's there, because I don't in the least concern myself as to what it feels like to be the loser, and because it's fun and I get what I want, or think I do. The more I am punished the more it gives me license to spite 'them'. The more kind people are to me, the more I despise them for being weak.

What is needed is for the delinquent somehow to gain sufficient fulfillment, sufficient *self*-esteem, sufficient respect, that he can begin to accept the needs of others and can find a way to gain what he wants in a manner that can increase his self-esteem. If he becomes a really good car mechanic he can take pride in his work and so can other people, then he does not need to be delinquent, for his skill has increased his stature rather than his delinquency diminished it.

The techniques that are incorporated in the *Children and Young Persons Act* are designed with these ideas in mind. It is very difficult to know at what point to increase the limits set upon a child by, for instance, depriving him of his liberty, and at what point to enable him to explore his potential by offering him facilities for this.

The statistics for juvenile crime however do offer us some clues. It is now by and large possible to build up a profile of a child's chances of being delinquent based upon certain factors. Some of these are as follows:

(a) It seems to matter a good deal how big his family is. (If there are more than four children he will be *more* likely to be delinquent.)

(b) It matters where he lives. Overcrowded urban areas in certain places add particular hazards.

(c) It matters which school he goes to. If a random group of children go to two schools in the same area (and those children randomized in relation to street, family size, income, etc.) then one school may have more delinquents than the other.

(d) It matters what the home circumstances are. If the father is absent, ill, apathetic or aggressive or delinquent, or the mother over-worked, inadequate, etc., the children will be more delinquent.

(e) There is a high correlation between illiteracy and delinquency. This, of course, is multi-factorial. The child may have a slightly low IQ and come from a semi-literate home, being one of five or six children. He may scarcely ever go to school but roam the streets with a gang of like-minded children, so that the illiteracy factor represents more the way the child reacts to his circumstances than either his intelligence or the standards of his school.

I believe we have two interwoven tasks to perform in relation to this group of delinquents. We must do all in our power to prevent the crime happening, both by increasing the proportion of crimes solved by the police and by making the child understand that we won't stand for it. It is useless simply to sit back and say, oh how dreadful, but poor lad, he's not depraved he's deprived. We must *also*, which is good parenting, show the child that nevertheless we respect him as an individual and wish him well. We must endeavour to increase the value he can gain from life. We should offer him more *good* things – education he really understands, enjoyment and exercise and exploration that he can experience, we must give him an opportunity to identify with the stable, the caring and the healthily masculine and help him to gain further self-esteem *after* this, by helping other people. In this way he will eventually grasp the meaning of conscience and collaboration. I believe that we may have trapped ourselves by our own liberality. Children *do* need us to understand their pain and try and rectify it, but they also need to know that we care for them enough and ourselves enough to set limits past which they cannot go.

(3) The neurotic – It is difficult to separate entirely the various groups of delinquents and the one spreads into the other, but there is a definite group of young people who are in very great confusion, under stress at home or at school, who can only try and escape this by delinquent acts. They know what they do is wrong, they know it is hurtful to others, they know that it is a self-defeating device, but nevertheless they are driven towards this method of expressing their unhappiness.

A girl who was normally quite sensible, though quiet, became very restless in class. She stopped lessons, became irritable and truculent. Her behaviour became more and more tiresome. A member of the staff asked what the trouble was; she responded by being extremely rude and turned her back. She would have outbreaks of rage when she threw books across the room and smashed a window.

She was the eldest daughter of a fairly large family. Her mother had recently had a baby. The father earned fairly good wages but was very aggressive, particularly when drunk. The mother told me she couldn't understand why her daughter was like she was, all she could say was it must be the school, they'd got a down on the child, they picked on her, blamed her for everything and made her very unhappy. Why – at home she was smashing. In fact had been a real little mother while baby was born and mother and baby been in hospital for some weeks, because of the mother's severe toxaemia which could have killed her. The mother concluded that the best thing would be for the daughter to stop at home for a bit and then try and get a new school for her. The daughter sat quite still during this interview, chewing gum and staring out of the window. I asked for her comments and she just muttered she didn't know.

After her mother had gone, I remarked that it might be quite hard struggling with a load of kids, worrying about her mother's health and perhaps with a rather difficult dad to handle; that perhaps if you've *got* to take on a great burden at home the only way to let off steam would be to blow off at school. She became quite amiable after this – and said she really didn't mind school and was surprised I'd said that, she'd dreaded coming to see me, thinking I'd 'put her away'. I said I thought when you were nearly grown up it was often hard not to be a bit childish at times when it was all hard work at home and no time to be a kid, just having to keep the others in order. We had a long and easy conversation and eventually she decided that she would, when things got too difficult, go and see the school nurse, whom she liked and trusted, rather than trail down to see me.

Jack came into juvenile court having snatched an old lady's shopping basket from her – taken the purse out of it and thrown the rest over a wall. He was twelve years old. He had been in court many times before, generally for stealing. He had been under supervision, he had been in Care and away at a community home from which he constantly absconded.

He had been remanded in Care and we had the benefit of numerous reports, psychiatric, psychological, social work and school. He had had a very sad history. A friend of his had died under his eyes. His parents had left their home to try and set up again away from disturbance and difficulties. They were Irish. The lad was small for his age, lively and everyone felt a loveable though disturbed child. When I said to him that he was making it difficult for us to help him, he said 'Well, why can't you put me away where I can't do it, you know if I'm in a Home I'll run away, you know if I'm around I'll do it again and again, why can't you *stop* me?' This boy with a tragic background had, I think, the typical neurotic response to his problem. He desperately needed help. He was frightened of aggression and yet used aggressive acts to draw attention to himself in an effort to be given limits that prevented him from these acts. He certainly demanded understanding, he certainly needed therapy so that he could gain trust in his own responses and those of the outside world, but it is arguable that until he could gain inner peace and control it would be too worrying for him to be at the mercy of his impulses, impulses with a core of health in that vaguely he was seeking a resolution to his anxieties, but with no possible benefit to him. A secure environment was therefore essential to him while his personal confusion was dealt with. I don't think it fair on children of this type to collude with their problem by endlessly 'excusing' it. Their need is to be helped to stop the delinquent activity and to gain normal healthy self-discipline so that they can then proceed to a happier life.

Joe took cars. A number of boys take cars. Sometimes, as I have suggested it's 'for fun', sometimes with a total disregard for other people's feelings and needs. Joe had at first joined a gang of lads and quite enjoyed the 'fun', but the normal responses of the court had no effect upon him. He eventually was remanded for reports and went to a community home for a while. However, his father asked to have him back. This was a very positive move as it was the first time his father had shown interest in Joe.

Joe's parents had separated some years ago. The father had moved away. Joe and his mother lived together alone and the boy had been a good son to her during a long period of bitterness and poverty. She had then found another man. Joe hated his step-father. He would run away from home, come back, row, run away again. It was at about this time he began to take cars.

When he was in the community home his father re-appeared and was upset that he had shown so little interest in the boy. He was now much more settled and longed to 'make it up to him'. Joe was delighted, he went home and, of course, all went well at first. Gradually, however, Joe began testing his father by being angry and difficult, the father was disappointed and became angry also, and Joe returned to his mother. His mother was at this time experiencing problems with her new husband. Joe was in despair. He didn't get on with his father, he couldn't bear to see his mother so upset. He took yet another car and again was sent away from home. It came to his notice that his mother was ill. He absconded from the home, took a car, dashed to his mother, crashed the car and again landed in court.

These cases, I hope, illustrate the 'neurotic' response of adolescents to their problems. The response is unsuitable and unacceptable. The children need a considerable amount of help so that their response to pain can better be understood.

Truanting

In Great Britain, as in most other countries, we firmly believe that it is our children's right to be educated. At a time when very few were, and they, the children of the well-to-do well-wishers set up little schools to offer the poor the advantages of learning. As a result of the industrial revolution, it became more and more necessary for work-people to read and write and do sums. It was also deemed appropriate to extend the function of the church to include 'Sunday schools', when children could be told the bible stories and given some understanding of religion. This was a far cry from the present time when not only is it a child's right to have education from the age of five till sixteen, but also it is enjoined upon him. In fact, it is so much enjoined upon him that if he does *not* go, he may be sent away from home (having committed no crime).

It's very tempting to wonder whether we really *are* doing the best for our children in insisting they stay at school for what on earth would they do otherwise? But it's quite salutary to examine illiteracy figures and also truanting figures in Great Britain. I have many opinions concerning education, and have no right to any of them, but I think *all* adults should review constantly their assumption as to what is right for other people so that they may be more just and more sensible.

There are a number of reasons why children don't go to school, some potentially healthy, some not.

71

(1) My family, and probably yours, was sufficiently highly motivated toward school and sufficiently in control of *me* that not only did I *go*, I also believed it was, if not 'doing me good' then preparing me for the future, or at any rate, it was impossible to conceive of not going, although I can't say I awfully enjoyed it. But if a family can't see the point of it (having gained not much themselves by going) or if they have no control over their children's behaviour and are exhausted and indifferent to their needs, then where is the motivation?

(2) Therefore it may be that the situation of school has to find ways to encourage children so that they will find the place so much better than being at home or roaming the streets, that they will come happily and eagerly. (I think Shakespeare had something to say about this.) A very large number of children are impatient people, not very able to take personal responsibility for their actions and it is very easy for a child *not* to go if there's something else they'd rather do, or if they want to gain status with a gang and are enjoined by that gang not to go. It is then fairly simple to blame the school for something not the school's fault. When a boy leaves school and gets a job, he may find that the standard of work, time-keeping and behaviour is far higher than that of the school, to his immense surprise and he can then either get the sack or pull his socks up. Eventually he may gain internal discipline by constantly losing jobs and yet wanting pay, but schools don't offer, except to the intellectual, any obvious immediate benefits, so it's easy to dismiss them as useless.

I think teachers get very dismayed that although they work extremely conscientiously to produce a time-table, an environment, a class atmosphere, that is lively, exciting and challenging, yet some students don't respond and still say school is awful. Perhaps we should accept that some always will and that although we want the best for the children, yet we are part of a system that we may approve of, and yet they may not. This is one of the disappointments of all paternalistic situations.

(3) There is no doubt, however, that some schools are better than others and in a few schools where it seems as though the teacher is there because she hates children and the cold, dank, uncaring, primitive, prison-like atmosphere reinforces this, it is a surprise that children go at all. The young of today are up against a pretty fierce society and perhaps if we let schools

encourage children to learn to be more responsible, more decision-makers, more the initiators then more children might go regularly to school, and gain from so doing.

(4) Bunking off from school is fun – it's daring, and offers a sense of adventure. Like all daring it can become stale and it can become dangerous. After the excitement is over, then wandering the streets can be boring, so that it is understandable that there is a very real threat that the truanter will become delinquent. On the whole, I don't think a normal child, truanting sometimes, becomes delinquent because he's truanting. He is likely to be delinquent as *well* as being a truanter, though obviously some children do both for a while, and then find that school is preferable and return.

(5) *School-leavers:* The last year at school always presents problems – when children stayed till 14, then 15 and now 16, there were difficulties too – and it is very hard to persuade a student who is *not* intellectual, who has no motivation for learning, who cannot see *what* he learns as of any relevance *nor* as any preparation for later life, to stay in school. Socially deprived youngsters tend to see contentment in materialist terms and therefore see adult status in terms of money, jobs, and leaving school. They find that they need immediate gratification and pleasure and this they can't get at school, so they leave. It is, it seems to me, an impossible conundrum to solve. It is against the law to work, it is against the law not to be at school, even if the student is *in* school, he may be aggressive, rude, noisy and impossible to teach. No wonder teachers turn a blind eye to the school truanter in this age group. Perhaps some degree of blind-eyeing is the best democratic method – so long as it is not too obvious. I think that by having a system where children can be brought to court for non-attendance we do in fact improve attendance for a number of children if not all in that our assumption that they *do* go has a general effect upon most.

(6) *The school refuser:* Some children get bullied at school or feel friendless or feel depressed and frightened and, not knowing why, think it's the school that is the problem. In a proportion of these children, a kindly and firm Education Welfare Officer, an intelligent and perceptive teacher, can help the child to return, can perhaps find ways to change the curriculum, or the teacher or the manner in which the child is treated. If the child is out

of school for long, the task of returning him becomes more and more difficult, and I am certain that, rather than let things drag on for term after term, we should bring our energies to bear very early on. In studies of school refusing cases, it has been found that a very high proportion began in primary school. Leaving a child for a year or two without doing much except indicate he ought to go, does no service to the child.

Some children fairly suddenly break away from regular attendance and begin absences. In a number of cases, as we have seen, there is no problem within the child of any great significance, but in some the absence may reflect some crisis or conflict which has fairly recently upset the family. Parents separate, or become depressed, or ill – fathers change jobs, or get another woman, or go to prison – mothers have babies, become unhappy – all factors which could disrupt an adolescent's sense of security absolutely fundamentally.

Lastly, during the crisis of early adolescence the child, being vulnerable, and sensitive to his family's situation and his own feelings, may become totally phobic about school. There is no external reason. He may have friends and like the staff, yet he cannot go. In these cases, it is urgent that the child should be seen as reponding to some overwhelming internal conflict usually connected with personal anxiety, such as exam neurosis, but often with a member of the family.

A girl could not go to school – nothing could get her there – yet she kept promising and promising she'd go. She came to juvenile court. She was in tears and so was her mother. They both promised she'd go but she couldn't. Eventually a report was asked for by a psychiatrist. It became very plain that the girl had an extremely psychologically ill mother and it was anxiety over this that stopped her going. It would seem, superficially, that it would have been nicer for her to be in school away from her mother, but the girl's anxiety could not allow this. School phobia is often a symptom not that the child hates school, but hates her home and it is for *this* she can't leave it. The girl I describe went, crying and lamenting, to a children's home. When she came back to court, she was a different child, and she came up to the bench and whispered to us 'don't let me go back home, let me go back to the children's home, *please*, it's so nice there'. It was her *mother* who could not bear the separation, not her.

Therefore in asking oneself the question, how do I deal with a child who doesn't go to school I have to remind myself that the problem is multi-factorial. A teacher it would seem to me, *a priori*, must first accept the principle that all children should go to school. She may not entirely agree with the law, but she must act within it, resign and/or try to change it, but it does no good to operate against it.

Secondly, a teacher should, I suppose, examine her own school as an institution and ask herself whether it seems to operate for the sake of the children or the staff. (One medical student I knew once suggested that many ward sisters act upon the assumption that the ward would work far more efficiently if it weren't for the patients.) If the school seems genuinely to *like* children and to work toward understanding their needs, then, assuming the teacher also likes the children, she could look at the methods of the school, and she should work, if possible, in a school whose philosophy she agrees with.

Most children are uneasy when there are no limits set in the school, no rules, no restrictions. Their sense of both omnipotence and of frailty, gives them anxiety – if there are no rules they may become too destructive, or others may become destructive to them. Neither do they want too many restrictions that are meaningless and reduce their ability to be self-organizing and self-reliant, whatever system of rules exist, some children will at some time try to break them because they are there – nevertheless, they feel safer in a moderately well-organized school, than in an anarchic one. They also need a teacher to be in control – not bossy and restrictive, but clearly in charge and relaxed, flexible but clear in her own mind what she wants. Children need to experiment, test and learn responsibilty as well as chemistry, so that reality testing is essential. If it is the law that you must go to school, it's not very helpful to a child if nobody seems to care if he goes or not, and hardly notices whether he exists when he is there. This is why I think that it does help to bring parents and children to court. It helps them to recognize that adults mean what they say.

Thirdly, she should take a look at her own feelings about the children and the school. Everyone has a right to enjoy their work and a school where the majority of teachers are having a bad time, is a bad institution. If children behave outrageously to a teacher, it may be because the school is an unhappy one, or the teacher unhappy or the children unhappy, and it is as well to accept one's own need for pleasure and reasonable return for one's efforts.

Fourthly, one looks at the child, sometimes the very fact that one *does* pay attention to the child has an effect, and certainly in some of the situations described that may account for non-attendance at school, the attentiveness of the teacher has been a partial solution. Clearly not always.

Mavis was fat, fifteen, disliked, a non-reader and a non-attender. In class she never said a word, just sat feeling miserable, helpless and angry. She got very bad marks, and was never asked a question as she was more or less forgotten. The others in the class said she was barmy and teased her. She responded by making matters worse. She was angry with the children and said that even if she did speak the teacher was sarcastic. She felt she would never catch up, never be liked, never be pretty and never be thin. So she stopped going to school. She hated it and it frightened her. She had a difficult relationship at home and the more she tried to slim the more her mother complained of the cost of the diet. When Mavis gained a bit more self-esteem and tried to be independent a little more, her mother couldn't bear it, quarrelled with her and Mavis responded by eating more and getting fatter. The few times she went to school the others teased her and she was even farther behind. When she didn't go to school, her mother nagged her. Somehow she needed to get some self-esteem. She couldn't slim, her mother found it impossible to let her, so she needed to be able to read. Remedial teaching was given to Mavis and the school alerted on her behalf. She was given, by her tutor, a placement at a day nursery and much enjoyed it. Very gradually, over more than a year, with outside counselling, remedial teaching and extra attention from the tutor, Mavis began to feel better. Her attendance picked up, her reading and writing improved and she even smiled sometimes. Now she goes regularly and is tackling the weight problem. Mavis is an example of a multi-factorial problem. Her non-reading, fatness and general misery stemmed initially from a very difficult attachment to her mother. The result at school was to establish a spiral of failure at every level – the teachers, pupils and family all disliked Mavis and despaired of her and none so much as Mavis herself. The counsellor refused to accept this picture of a miserable fat girl and helped Mavis to feel more aware of her part in the spiral. The remedial teacher gave her personal attention and reading skills, the tutor a really enjoyable out-of-school activity and gradually Mavis *had* to stop being sorry for herself, for there was very little left to be sorry about. She is now going to stay at school into the VIth form and do an 'O' level or two and people seem quite to like her.

A girl came to see me with a small problem not in any way connected with school life. I did ask her which school she attended, however, and she said that although she wasn't quite 16, the 'free school' she had attended had asked her to leave to 'make room' for another girl who had greater problems than she had. She added that although she had not attended her ordinary school much, she loved the free school, partly because they did things she really thought useful for the future, partly because they had selected her when there was a long waiting list. She came back to see me a few weeks later to say she was now back at the 'free' school as they had a vacancy and would stay to complete her course and then get a job. In another 'free' school the intake is very local, based upon a few streets and the children come either because their friends have told them about it, or because their parents have met someone 'in the flats' who knows of it. Can it be that school attendance would improve if child and parent had very real and local choice, and if the parents were genuinely more involved in selection and in the school activities, including using it themselves for learning purposes?

If children and parents believe a school to be a place you have to go to whether you will like it or not, and particularly if the parent has had a bad experience in schooling himself, is it surprising that the family colludes in the child's perception that school is a kind of prison, holding him in and preventing him from enjoying life and becoming an adult?

REFERENCES

5. *Larkrise to Candleford.* Flora Thompson. Now in Penguin.
6. *Adolescent Boys in East London.* Peter Wilmott. Penguin 1969.

CHAPTER 7

The role of the teacher

Primarily of course the function of a school is to educate. The interpretation of this function varies very much indeed. I doubt if many schools really believe that teaching consists solely of the offering of information to a child in order that he may fill his head with facts useful or otherwise, take exams and leave better prepared to tackle life. Nearly all teachers recognize that education involves a process of growth within the child and that that growth is not simply a growth of the mind but of the whole person, so that, hopefully, the child leaves school more able to be self-reliant, clear thinking and more understanding of himself and others. Even if the interpretation of education was fairly narrow, it is now generally accepted that there are times in a child's life where he unexpectedly perhaps fails to be able to use what is offered him appropriately. Children have learning blocks; some children find one subject more difficult than another; some hate exams; some after a fairly tranquil period of learning, find themselves panicking over homework or unable to complete essays, commit work to memory or in some other way seem unable to study. In this book I have discussed to some extent, normal adolescence and have also focused upon particular symptoms that some young people exhibit. Bad behaviour, drug taking, delinquency, pregnancy, tearfulness and inability to come to school. I will not deal at length with learning difficulties as I am not an educational psychologist, but I think that even if school-teachers really do believe that their task is to instruct the pupil and not to understand him, yet if the pupil cannot seem to use instruction they would want to know why. Therefore it would seem to me that teachers do need to know something about what may affect young people's learning ability even though they may believe that the pupil's behaviour is best dealt with in terms of discipline or kindness.

Once the classroom becomes as it were a life-learning room, the teacher is far more exposed. The young people can test her more severely and can give her far more feelings of helplessness, anger and anxiety. If a class is securely fastened, as it were, to its seats and the teacher to his blackboard, discipline is relatively easy though the whole ambience must be pretty sterile. In an odd way, some children feel safer in this situation partly because they are so afraid of their own lack of internal discipline that they need external limits to be pretty fierce, but it does mean that the teacher has to withdraw as a person to an extent and not come too close to the pupil. It is obviously far better from a truly educative point of view if this static, life denying situation is replaced by something more like a healthy society. If a teacher can come to meet the real needs of the class and the pupils learn that they are respected as people, then a trusting relationship can be established. The teacher can know as a good parent can, that adolescents do need and appreciate some limits – for as we have suggested, they are very unnerved by a curious mixture of apprehension over their powerful and aggressive feelings and their sense of helplessness. They are frightened of chaos, because they feel chaotic and the more chaos a teacher lets them show, the more scared they may become. In the end, they can learn that they have developed inner controls that give them a sense of safety even when there are no outer controls, but very many young adolescents, particularly those brought up in chaotic, uncaring or aggressive households can only at first respond to freedom by abusing it. Thus they either turn the class into a disorganized nightmare or group with others to torment the teacher or some scapegoat among themselves. It is enormously helpful to young people to find that adults themselves are so confident about their own inner controls that they can contain anger and spite and stand up to bursts of aggression and wild behaviour without either unleashing fury themselves or appearing panic-stricken. Said another way, young people want to be shown that they are not omnipotent and that they cannot damage adults or others by the fury of their own feelings. Eventually a class can become self-disciplined partly by feeling safe with the teacher and partly by discovery of a group need to co-exist. Very destructive and angry young people may have to be removed from a class if it is seen that the group cannot, without losing its own sense of self-esteem, contain them. I don't think it appropriate for a class to have to cease to function as a learning group in order constantly to attend to the needs and behaviour of a member who cannot be controlled in a normal way, and I believe that if the students are helped in this kind of decision it will

79

relieve a great deal of anxiety.

Perhaps far more important to discuss is the fact that as the teacher, as it were, enables the class to become more free, then she will be brought into other areas of her pupils' lives. They will expose more of their feelings and more of their needs. Young people are thinking a lot about their problems and about the future. Given a chance they will talk; they will talk not only to their friends but to the teachers they trust. Some will choose one teacher, some another.

It is obviously easier to confide in someone if there is some degree of shared experience. Craft teachers and, of course, home economics teachers, by having actual contact in a shared task, can offer to the pupil a degree of privacy within the actual teaching situation. Many pupils confide in teachers who have more formal contact during class but who for some reason seem to be safe people. I think though, that handicrafts, cooking, sewing and other creative pursuits do in fact offer young people a quality of experience much nearer to a homelike situation, and because of this, the pupil and the teacher both take up roles more like parent-child than in any other school occupation. Pupil and teacher are sharing a task and at the same time the pupil must share the teacher with other pupils, so that the feelings evoked within a family are more nearly established. The attention seeking, envious or dispirited and unloved, all may get a chance or hope to. The teacher then becomes the focus of the young person's feelings and can be used (at times very dramatically). This poses problems for the teacher. She may feel very aware that there is not enough time for her to give the pupil the help she needs. She may feel she has not the skill and may worry that she will make matters worse. There may be problems of confidentiality or of dual loyalties.

I have dealt to an extent with the problem behaviour of pupils, but now we are dealing with another situation. The pupil has made some decision that she will trust a teacher and ask for help. It may be that the teacher has made it easier for her to do this by establishing that she is approachable and by indicating at times that she recognizes that the pupil may have a problem. It is sometimes quite hard to achieve a balance with a distressed girl between offering help and appearing to pry, and many teenagers both long to confide and long for privacy at the same time.

Frequently they approach their problem crab-wise, not daring to establish with anyone what it's all about in case there is an over-response or a rejection. Frequently the client hardly knows where the problem really lies. She is confused, troubled, perhaps anxious and sleepless, but attaches all these symptoms to something irrelevant 'If only I had less/more homework I wouldn't have a headache/worry over exams/burst into tears'; 'If only I didn't get such backache/feelings of tiredness/acne/ . . .'; 'If only I were more popular/had a real friend/wasn't bullied/. . . .' It may be that it will take some time measured not in hours but in days or weeks before a distressed teenager can dare approach a member of staff and talk about her real anxieties. People cannot be hurried. They have, first of all to perceive that they have difficulties and then to attempt to deal with them on their own. If they cannot find a solution they may talk with their friends. If they then reach the conclusion that they must talk to some adult (particularly if that adult has indicated that she can listen and that she recognizes there is some problem) then at last people can bury some of their fears and attempt to accept help. Adults cannot and must not solve problems for adolescents. It's so easy to 'know best' but it must always be remembered first that we have no right to decide for anyone how they should act and second that the adolescent (and for that matter the adult) grows in maturity and strength by meeting a crisis, and taking responsibility for solving it. The adult is used as a temporary support and as a mature person who may enable the adolescent to see his alternatives, understand his feelings, accept reality, better than he could before.

When therefore a teacher moves from the position of educator to that of advisor and subsequently counsellor, it is quite a profound move. Generally in teaching we know the answer, have facts at our finger-tips and hope the pupil will learn from our information enough to help him to think and utilize what has been given him.

Counselling is different. We don't know the answers. We may think we do, in that we tend to view a problem as though it is our own and base our advice upon that. There is an added quality to the situation. The student likes us enough to give us his trust; this makes us feel good. We then give back of our best to help him. If he can't or won't take our advice it is very easy to feel rejected and to become angry or disappointed. Again we, being human, respond in different ways. Some problems upset us very much and others not so much. We may respond strongly to some statement, not because, *per se*, it is of greater import than another, but because it has a greater effect upon us. We may also like one pupil better than another. That pupil may call up in us feelings that are rather unexpected. It is very useful when trying to understand what occurs in any communication to remember that each party brings their own personality into the contact and their own expectations as to how the other will respond. An adolescent may find it hard to see the counsellor as the person she really is, but project on to her a super-imposed image based upon previous experience, upon hidden anxieties.

One of my clients constantly said to me 'You're different today, you seem more bored, you don't seem interested in me. I can't talk while you are so different'. In fact I was exactly the same, but she was struggling at that time with a very powerful recognition that she needed my support. She longed to trust me, but when she was a child she had always failed in her attempts to get support from her mother. Her father was a pretty sick man and her mother very depressed. Isabel, my client, always felt that the whole thing was her fault and indeed if she did approach her mother she would frequently get a reply such as '. . . and look what you've done to your father with all your moans' or 'well I'll try and help but I've got so much on my hands dealing with your father . . .' Isabel could not believe that I could respond in a different way so that she felt that I was moving away from her whenever she was coming up to meet some pretty fundamental anxieties.

There is another trap, I think; young people who have not had really secure relationships with parents in childhood, especially those brought up in establishments where it is impossible to relate to one stable person, find all encounters difficult. They may be very friendly and talkative, but they are unable to develop any deep relationship either with their own age group or with an adult. But each time they meet somebody new because they desperately need something less shallow and more important, they believe that this time it will work. It does not because it cannot. Deprived young people are very difficult to work with. A compassionate counsellor, recognizing how empty they are, may find great satisfaction in making friends but inevitably the counsellor will be disappointed.

Karen came to see me after having had an abortion. She talked to me very freely about her family (who were useless), her school (which was awful), and her social worker (who was an old frump). She remarked that she was so very glad to have come to see me, that she'd never realized anyone existed with whom she could talk so easily. My first reaction, of course, was of delight. I then realized that it would do that girl no service if I accepted her statement completely, because then she would have to fail me in the future. She would be no more likely to relate to me than she had been to all other people. She might also find herself quite frightened that she could not be angry with me as a method of dealing with her despair, thus finding it more difficult to come back to see me. It was therefore necessary to help her to see that while I was pleased at her visit and her ability to discuss problems with me, yet I understood that getting to know people well might be quite hard for her. I also had to convey that nevertheless I'd like to see her again and that we would only talk in the future about things she wished to discuss. I let her know that she might find it hard to return to someone she'd talked very freely with. One visit does not make a relationship, but if one can accept what has been given and expect very little for the future, then these empty and deprived girls may slowly build a relationship of a kind that they can · acknowledge without too much anxiety.

The very shy are also difficult to help. One reason for shyness lies in the inability to express angry or demanding feelings. If a teacher questions a shy person she may only respond by saying 'leave me alone' or by decrying any problem. It takes a long time for a shy, unhappy, friendless person to accept that she *can* relate to anyone. That, after all, is her problem. The teacher or counsellor may have to be very gentle, slow, undemanding. It may be at first that 'non-verbal' communication is the only method possible, a gentleness of tone or a request for col- laboration in a task. But shy people don't need 'mothering', perhaps the reverse. Although they would wither away if one · were hearty and demanding, the 'come on, girl, what about a laugh?' approach, yet they don't want a 'poor little love, I realize how scared you are' method. They will affect us one way or the other according to our natures because by making us anxious we will respond in the way other people have in the past (which confirms the girl in her attitude). Therefore, we neither pry, over-encourage nor mother, what we should do is to recognize how helpless we feel about the girl and wonder how she has achieved that feeling in us, for it may give us a clue as to what *she* is frightened of. Generally, it is of discovery. The shy girl is frightened that we will discover her true nature and is frightened of self-discovery – she is often an angry and fairly strong person actually and our job is to enable her to feel confident that it's all right for her to be as noisy and aggressive and demanding as other people and that she will not be destructive or destroyed.

A girl came to see me complaining of shyness when in a group situation. She was a student and had good relationships with individuals and her boy-friend. At her college it was the practice to hold groups to discuss ideas and plan projects. Catherine was completely tongue-tied. She said her mind went blank and she felt awful. I discovered that in fact although she had initially said that she had a good relationship with a boy, it was based on a curiously childlike behaviour pattern. They spoke baby-language and never really talked about anything serious nor quarrelled nor allowed themselves to feel strongly. Catherine had always been shy and quiet. Oddly she was quite demanding with me after her first few interviews (she had, in fact, come to see me upon another matter). I felt that this girl was hiding from me and from herself, considerable strength, imaginative powers and ability to organize and I told her so. Gradually we unravelled things until she was able to discover that she had held back the recognition of strength because of a long-lasting anxiety, concerning sibling rivalry (closely linked with a vague recognition of difficulties between her mother and father) and that she had almost consciously chosen a boy who would collude in her need to appear like a baby because of problems of his own. Soon she demanded more of herself and other people. She obtained a very good scholarship to study further, her boy-friend could not keep up with her new maturity, but they remained friendly and Catherine became self-confident and able to trust her own opinions. Many a shy person is almost literally hiding behind mother's skirts, fearful of emerging lest she be too strong, not too weak.

Nevertheless, the quiet, withdrawn pupil may be very depressed or feel very anxious. There is a distinction to be made. Shy people can usually work well enough, but not join in or contribute. Depressed people cannot. Depressed people are often called lazy.

They are apathetic, complain they are tired, do very little work and frequently tell you to 'leave them alone' yet they do need help. If a teacher can indicate that she recognizes there is a problem and that she can wait until the pupil is ready to talk about it then very often that pupil can feel safe to bring herself into a helping situation. As I have already mentioned the initial statement of the problem may have little bearing upon the actual one, but is a safe beginning. I find that if someone complains of laziness or tiredness, it often helps by saying that one often feels like that *because* one is working hard at something else in one's mind that doesn't seem to be coming out right – which offers the pupil an opening, so that rather than saying 'why are you so lazy or apathetic?' or 'why don't you ever complete essays any more?' or 'can't you tell me what's up, you never used to be like this?' one might suggest to her that often people *do* get stuck at times because other things are occupying them. Adolescence is an extremely confusing and busy time. The task of finding independence and an understanding of one's own nature, a good deal of contradictory feelings and thoughts must be endured. It is a shame in some ways that so much has to be done at once. Careers envisaged, ideologies established, sexual feelings understood, relationships experienced, parents accepted as ordinary people, body image, gender role, drives and needs – all the complexities of the human condition acknowledged.

Adolescents are a moody group: they are marvellously happy one day and hopelessly depressed the next, active and subsequently exhausted, eager and the apathetic, but a teacher, seeing a young person day after day, soon recognizes a vast and long continued change in mood and can be available to give help if need be.

CHAPTER 8

Whose responsibility ?

Children show their problems in many ways, as we have seen. Some are quiet and shy, or tearful and withdrawn. Some are aggressive and rude or insolent. Some have vast mood swings. Others are anxious, overconcerned over homework and exams, some apathetic and 'lazy'. Some daren't do gym and take their clothes off, some daren't go to school or won't go to school. Some get into gangs, other are 'loners'. Some are teachers' pets, others the despair of teachers. Some take pills or sniff glue, or steal, or get pregnant or pick a fight. Some attempt suicide or run away from home. Some have frequent headaches, sore throats and painful periods. It all sounds pretty confused and pretty frightful. How can it be dealt with? I hope I have shown some of the reasons for the various symptoms I have listed and indicated to a degree how they might be handled, but if in a fairly average class with a good teacher in a pleasant school, problems insist on existing, who should deal with them?

It's a helpless feeling when one uses all the skill one has in dealing with a child who either has a problem or is a problem without anything apparently happening to show that it's made things better, and it is tempting to blame either the child for refusing to be helped, or oneself for one's lack of skill or the school for not offering enough time. Practically all the problems met with in adolescence in a school can be dealt with or at least contained by the ordinary people who make up a school society. Most problems of out of school can be dealt with there and then by ordinary caring people, particularly if that society is a fairly healthy one. I think it's easy to assume (with humility) that a problem can only be solved by somebody called an 'expert'.

I don't think people, and particularly teachers, recognize what enormous skills they have themselves. Teachers see and deal with far more adolescents than any expert. No doctor, psychotherapist or analyst has anything like the experience and skill of a teacher. She is right there with pupils all the time. Some teachers manage to put up such barricades between themselves and their pupils that they have never experienced them in effect – but surely these are rare?

If a teacher is capable of watching and listening then most young people will be capable of sharing *in their own time*. If she is not frightened of controlling her class, most children will feel safe. If she is capable of giving children the opportunity to be self-reliant most children will be so. But a few will stand out as being different; sadder, worse behaved or more anxious. I believe that the best person to help a child is that person she knows best at least at *first*. If the problem does not seem to be getting better then the teacher can discuss with the child the great value of taking the problem elsewhere. It must never be forgotten that if this conclusion is reached then several new factors must be considered.

If a teacher feels secure enough in her own skills, then she can refer a child to someone else without feeling she herself has failed. Each one of us has different skills, none are better nor worse, nor more or less difficult. Sometimes I think teachers get a bit possessive about the children and can't believe that the counsellor or clinic can do 'their' child any good so they find referral very hard indeed. Others are so unaware of their own value that they refer everybody, when in fact they could do the child so much good themselves.

And what of the child? If an adolescent finally brings himself to talk a little it may well be an immense act of bravery. It may be that he is terrified that he is mad or something frightful. It may be that he has at last been able, for the first time in his life, to trust somebody enough to talk at all. If he then gets a response in effect that either he's too ill or too awful for the teacher to deal with, then how does he feel if he's told to go somewhere else? He may feel very angry, very rejected or very frightened.

At the Youth Counselling Centre where I work, we are in a mid-position here. We receive referrals and sometimes have to make referrals. The most successful clients are those who have decided to come upon their own initiative or who are helped to come by one of their own friends. Nevertheless some referrals *do* work.

I once saw a girl who was obviously extremely angry. She came with her mother who was very worried about her behaviour. After a while, when I suggested the mother sat outside, I put it to the girl that she must be resentful of coming as though her mother was punishing her. She agreed and said that what would be the use of attending because everything she said would go back to mum. We made a pact that I would never see her mother without her permission and that everything we said would remain confidential. Once or twice we saw the mother together, because in fact the girl needed desperately her mother's good-will – but we could never have reached this stage if I hadn't helped her to express her anger at coming in the first place.

A referral, therefore, is difficult for teacher and child and the feelings of both must be respected. A school counsellor, it would seem to me, can be immensely valuable if the teaching staff totally accept her as playing an important part in the life of the school, neither more nor less important than anyone else, but different. A teacher has a more direct contact with children, she is used to dealing with a group and although encouraging self-expression, yet controlling it lest it becomes too demanding at certain times. A counsellor need not be, nor should be, directive in the same way. It is her job to listen and to reflect, to help to open some more doors, and to help the child to gain more *self* knowledge. This takes time. Some people like working in class as teachers, some prefer counselling and there is no doubt that the skills are somewhat different. All human beings at times are teaching, or healing, or mothering, or listening, but we don't all pretend to be professionals, just humans. There is a very real skill in medicine, in teaching and in counselling and upon occasion these skills are needed. I honestly believe that a number of patients in a waiting room could be cured without a doctor, and I believe a number of troubled children can be cured without a psychotherapist, but how do we know which or whom? How to protect ourselves against the anxieties that flood us, once we begin to listen to the young?

If I were describing the ideal, I think, as far as schools were concerned, my ideal would be something like this:

I would take for granted that the teachers respected each other and the Head and had a common aim in their attitude to education, albeit with ample room for individuality and personal responsibility. I would like to be able to know that the children were given freedom to be themselves and in order to enable this to happen I would like to see the school as being a part of the community, so that parents were involved in the school,

88

consulted about their children, and respected in their ability to offer their own experience of their children. In this way the school could be a living extension of the home and the community. I would know that there would be problems, some among staff, some among children. I would like to see a pastoral care system that sensitively recognized early enough, signs and symptoms of trouble in a particular child. I would know that this sensitivity would produce added anxieties in the life of the teachers, so that I would have, within the school, a support structure which gave staff an opportunity to gain insight and strength so that they could help more children adequately themselves and be more confident in handling difficulties while recognizing which children might need further help.

I was asked by a tutor at a College of Further Education to assist her in discovering a method of helping the young students with their problems. This college seemed to attract a number of very disturbed adolescents whose problems seemed at times insurmountable. There was a very high proportion of drop-outs in the first term, which seemed wasteful of resources and sad for the students.

It seemed that some kind of counselling service might increase the ability of the students to use the college more effectively and to prevent such high wastage. We were able to receive a small grant from a charitable foundation in order to examine more closely what the situation really was.

We planned a questionnaire which was offered to all students attending for the first term to take up a full-time course that led toward 'O' level examination. The questionnaire was completed in the presence of the student by the researcher.

The questions were designed to elicit from the student with whom they lived, whether their family was complete, what type of school they had left and why. They were also asked their opinion of their school and of the college.

The research worker was a trained psychotherapist and was able to give us her private assessment of each student as a result of the interview. The students took a joint intelligence test, as well as having the interview here described.

I won't detail the results, but briefly we found the position to be this:

(a) The students were almost all seen as failures in their previous school, or had been expelled.

(b) The IQs of the students was surprisingly high (98% above average intelligence).

(c) They believed their previous school had failed them either because it was 'too posh and middle class', 'treated you as kids' or 'too restrictive and uninterested'.

(d) They had suffered in general a high degree of family disturbance.

(e) They felt proud of coming to the college. They said 'well you have to pass a test and I got in' and 'they treat you as adults here'. Perhaps they didn't realize that a very high proportion of applicants did get in, but nevertheless it may have been the first experience of success that many students had ever had.

(f) At the end of the first term without any counselling service being officially established, the fall-out rate dropped from the 30% of previous years to 15% and the exam results at the end of the year showed a positive upward move.

The interest shown by the research worker in each individual student *must* have had a very real effect upon his attitude to college.

(1) The role of the counsellor would be to support the staff who deal with the face-to-face problems in the classroom and who may have anxieties concerning particular children's behaviour. To increase their confidence in their handling of the children and to enable them to recognize when a child needs further help. To discuss with staff matters such as confidentiality within the school and in relation to parents.

(2) The counselling of individual children or handling of groups if thought useful. The diagnosis of problems beyond the school counsellor's role, referral and discussion with agencies involved.

(3) Close liaison with the members of staff of the school, the education welfare officers, social workers, school doctors and treatment agencies within the community, particularly th educational psychologist and the Child Guidance Clinic.

(4) A boy called Jack attended a College of Further Education. He had been referred by his social worker to the college. He lived in a therapeutically oriented hostel at first, but later moved into rooms. His parents lived away from London. He had a very bad relationship with them and had become mildly delinquent. He had very great difficulty in settling down. He tended to become

very emotional, at times noisy, often very depressed. He would upon occasion take various drugs, including LSD and would be, of course, even more difficult to manage. At college he settled surprisingly well at first. The other students became quite fond of him and were very supportive and kind. He was placed in a tutorial class in the care of a highly skilled tutor. At the college there was a system whereby tutors and other teachers had the support of a weekly discussion with a consultant psychotherapist. There was also a counsellor who could see students who wished to make use of his services. The counsellor also had some teaching commitments.

Although Jack settled well at first in this very caring environment, yet it was quite obvious that he needed outside help. He was seen regularly in a counselling clinic. His behaviour in class gradually deteriorated. He made greater and greater demands upon the tutor and the students who frequently would stop work and either try to wake him up from his apathy or calm him from his wildness. The tutor described how helpless she felt in dealing with Jack. All her skills seemed to be useless; she felt very guilty and upset until she discussed the matter with the therapist. It was recognized that the tutor's primary role was to teach, that the other members of the group deserved to get what they had come for, education, and that this boy could not at that time profit from the college. Once the tutor had cleared her own mind and recognized that the college system, excellent as it was, could not cure a highly disturbed boy, she was able to recommend that he was asked to leave.

Jack was upset by this. He saw security in the college and was extremely dismayed and became very depressed. I discussed his feelings with him a good deal and, without the college's support he decided to go home for a while. He was able, after a few months, to recognize what he had contributed to the college's decision, applied to return and came back far more able to contain his feelings. So that, in fact, his dismissal had helped him to accept the reality of other people's needs but even if this had not been the case the college would have been correct in dismissing him. I think at times it has to be recognized that some children are, at a point in time, too disruptive or too ill for any counselling or tutorial system of a school to handle, unless that school is established as a therapeutic community. Nevertheless, a very high standard of care and containment is possible and can modify a surprisingly large proportion of the difficult behaviour patterns of children.

The counsellor

It is very difficult to determine the absolute needs in school for a counsellor. Schools vary so greatly, but if a counsellor is appointed then every member of the school should welcome the appointment. It is sad to have to recognize that this is not always the case. It may be that a counsellor is appointed because the Head thinks it a good idea or because she has had an uprush of problems in the school and is seeking ways of getting things back to normal; whatever the reason, the school staff, I think, should really know what the counsellor's function is and accept her as a valuable member of staff. Counsellors can have quite a bad time. I know of one school where the counsellor is left more or less on her own. She has a room at the top of the building which has an outside staircase, and is therefore more or less cut off from the classrooms. There is very little contact with teachers. Boys, some whom are very aggressive and disturbed, come to her eyrie. She has no telephone so that she is both geographically and psychologically isolated. The confidentiality problem is, of course, solved in this case, because no one sees the boys go up or down and scarcely anyone consults or sees the counsellor, but is this ideal? I think it may well express the attitude of the school towards counselling – 'we'd better have it, but it's a bit of a waste of time and gets in the way of teaching'. Confidentiality is, however, a great problem. I think it absolutely essential that material given in a counselling session should not be shared with anyone else whomsoever. If the counsellor believes that something that has been said *must* be shared with the Head or other teachers then the client must agree that this is so. In the same way I believe that no teacher or counsellor should discuss a pupil's confidences with a parent or anyone else without permission.

Nevertheless, and I think this is important, teachers find it very irritating that at times they discover by chance that a pupil is seeing a social worker or welfare officer or outside counsellor without their knowledge, if they are themselves deeply involved with or anxious about a child. Anyone has the absolute right to seek help from whom he likes and there are times when adolescents use one person after another to help them solve problems which is reasonable and understandable, nevertheless there are also occasions where it would be a great relief to an anxious teacher to know that a child is getting help, or even to know that odd behaviour in a child might be recognized by someone else as part of a family problem – I am not suggesting confidential material gets shared by all and sundry – quite the reverse, but I believe a child better served if social workers, welfare officers, doctor and teachers can collaborate with one another. This demands a recognition of each others skills and a trust that, alas, not all professional people have.

The child will soon sense that people are getting together and spilling private material to each other and sometimes an ill considered remark by a teacher will destroy a good relationship with a counsellor forever. But children are secretive and paranoid. They frequently assume that once a secret is stated it will travel like wildfire. They may well view a school counsellor as allied to the teachers and bound to tell the others everything that's been said, however private, hesitant or shameful, even if this is not the case. Children reckon that all teachers talk about them in the Staff Room (and they are right!) just as parents do at home – they find it very difficult to believe that their words could ever be privately contained.

Jennifer came to see me upon the advice of the school doctor. She had many problems of behaviour, learning and relationships. I asked her whether she had ever talked with the school counsellor – she said vehemently that she could *never* talk to him, her problem would be all over the school in no time. I was surprised as I knew him to be quite unlikely to do this. She said that when she first got to the school, the Head had given them a talk and introduced the counsellor to them and asked him to say a few words. He told the new pupils where his room was and that whatever the problem he'd be pleased to talk with them about it. He then gave one or two examples of the kind of difficulties some pupils had had. Jennifer said fiercely 'that shows you couldn't trust him – if he's going to tell all of us about other people, then he'll tell others all about me'. There is, therefore, it seems to me a need to emphasize confidentiality and a need to accept that some young people, frightened of their view of their own characters, might well find it very hard to bring themselves to speak at all.

I would suggest therefore that there should be alternatives to the school counsellor organization outside the school instead of inside, so that adolescents could choose for themselves the place where they felt most comfortable.

Adolescence is not a disease. It is a time of very great growth. I see it as a kind of kaleidoscope; the adolescent shifts position restlessly, different ephemeral patterns seem constantly to be emerging, but finally the scene settles and the picture becomes clear and more steady.

Very many adolescents are fairly happy, untroubled, easy to be with and relatively calm and peaceful, some are not. Some are apparently depressed or suicidal, lazy, scruffy, lonely, irritable, pig-headed, rude, aggressive, uncaring, selfish, narcissistic, silly; some are idealistic, unselfish, energetic, gay, loving, intelligent, excited, poetic; some are revolutionary or religious or drifting or delinquent. In fact all adolescents are a little of *all* these characteristics at some time, but a few are stuck at some point; they are genuinely depressed, genuinely so angry their aggression gets out of bounds, genuinely lonely, or impotent, or delinquent or anxious or suicidal. Nearly all of these can be helped because adolescence is such a growing point and so fluid. Some are pretty damaged by past events so that their personalities are likely to be forever some kind of problem. All adults and the adolescents themselves can help rather than hinder the normal process. We can do it by respecting them, by refusing to collude with their weaknesses. We should not allow our society to offer false solutions in the way of advertising the advantage of possessions, cigarettes, alcohol as a way of being happy. Neither should we entice them into revolutionary attitudes nor delinquent behaviour under cover of modernity. In schools we should constantly be aware that the child is a growing individual not a cypher in a uniform, we should work with them in their search for identity, offering them a framework but insisting on the importance of self-reliance.

Adolescents become adults; society will be formed by them. If we can help them to take responsibility for their own bodies, feelings and actions then we haven't done to badly. If, primarily, we instil in them a sense of *self-esteem* then we can leave them to recognize the reality of others' esteem.

You and I care for others because we were relatively well cared for ourselves. Young people *long* to like themselves, when they can they can love humanity and see to the making of a decent world.

94

What other agencies can help schoolchildren?

Education

(a) Education Welfare Officer combining, now, the function of the (London) Care Committee and the Attendance Officer. Staff are receiving more training than of old and can be of enormous help in cases where families and children are at risk, or children not attending school. Schools may vary a good deal in their attitude to, and collaboration with, these workers.

(b) Educational Psychologists. The amount of direct contact psychologists have with schools is extremely variable. If it is good, many children can be helped without needing to attend child guidance clinics.

(c) Child Guidance Clinics. These vary very much in resources. There is a rising interest in the problem of adolescents and a vast increase in some areas in the positive collaboration with schools.

Social problems

Some schools do have teachers visiting homes, but although a knowledge of family may be extremely useful it is possible that the Social Services Department already know certain families. If a child is on a Supervision Order, either because of delinquency or non-school attendance, then a social worker will in any case be involved. It is sometimes suggested that there is not sufficient contact between Social Workers, Educational Welfare Officers and school personnel, which is regrettable.

Delinquency

(a) Social workers are involved with delinquent children and act as liaison with families, schools, police and courts.

(b) The police now have a good deal of contact with schools and frequently have special projects to assist in educating children about the law; some work closely in local neighbourhood projects. The Juvenile Bureaux and the 'Caution' system bring the police very close to the families of children and with school and social workers.

(c) The NSPCC, of course, is still very active in most urban areas.

Youth clubs

The personnel of Youth Clubs frequently are interested in counselling individual children, are often involved in Intermediate Treatment Schemes (given as an Order as part of Supervision by Juvenile Courts). The Adventure Playground and detached Youth Work projects are particularly knowledgeable concerning some of the most vulnerable youngsters.

Special projects

Special projects particularly in urban settings, exist to help drifting young people, those running from home, homeless. In London the Soho, Blenheim, etc. projects are examples.

Counselling

(a) Family Planning advice can now be obtained from GPs as well as from Family Planning Clinics, free of charge, whether a girl is married or not. Several towns, however, have set up special clinics for young people, for example Brook Advisory Centres, etc.

(b) Pregnancy. GPs, Brook Advisory Centres, pregnancy centres, etc., deal with pregnancy problems. Addresses of these centres can be found in telephone books.

(c) General counselling. A number of 'open door' counselling agencies exist. Some are staffed by volunteers, some by partially trained and some by professionally trained personnel. The standards vary and the treatment varies. The Standing Conference for the Advancement of Counselling has now set up the British Association for Counselling in order, partly, to ensure recognized standards. The National Association of Young People's Counselling and Advisory Services links many organizations, offers conferences, and, via the National Youth Bureau in Leicester, publishes a regular journal and holds an information file containing addresses of services in Great Britain.

(d) The London Youth Advisory Centre is a general counselling service but has doctors as well as social workers on its staff. It offers a contraceptive service, counselling for pregnancy and psycho-sexual problems, as well as counselling upon school, family, relationship, work, etc., problems. LYAC keeps very close links with schools, social work departments, health visitors, etc., and organizes multi-disciplinary seminars.

Health

(a) The family doctor is not always used by adolescents who are a fairly healthy lot but suffer from psychological rather than health hazards. But many GPs now take a particular interest in the young. It may be that a special service on the lines of LYAC might be better used. Time will tell. The school doctor now sees her role far more in terms of discerning lack of adjustment to adolescence, rather than in detecting solely physical illness. Some school doctors have extra training for this purpose.

(b) Health Visitor, School Nurse. The health visitor, trained as she is to observe family interaction, is frequently well-trusted by young people and their parents. It may be that in future she will become more and more involved in handling adolescents within their family setting. The school nurse is in some schools used as a quasi-counsellor.